D1458737

BASIC BOOK OF
GARDEN PESTS
AND DISEASES

IN THE SAME SERIES

Chrysanthemum Growing
Dahlia Growing
Flower Gardening
Rock Gardens and Pools
Rose Growing
Vegetable Growing
Pruning
The Herbaceous Border
Weekend Gardening
Carnations and Pinks
Cloche and Frame Gardening
Natural Gardening: compost and 'no-digging'

BASIC BOOK OF GARDEN PESTS AND DISEASES

W. E. SHEWELL-COOPER

MBE, NDH, FRSL, DLitt, MRST, Dip. Hort. (Wye)

BARRIE & JENKINS
COMMUNICA-EUROPA

©W. E. Shewell-Cooper 1978

First published in 1978
by Barrie and Jenkins Ltd
24 Highbury Crescent, London N5 1RX

ISBN 0 214 20474 X

Printed litho in Great Britain
by W & J Mackay Limited, Chatham

Contents

List of illustrations 6
Preface 8
1 The pest and disease problem examined 9
2 Hygiene in the garden 15
3 Pests that attack plants generally 18
4 Diseases that attack plants generally 31
5 The pests of vegetables 34
6 The diseases of vegetables 51
7 The pests of flowers 74
8 The diseases of flowers 81
9 The pests of fruit 91
10 The diseases of fruit 120
11 The pests and diseases of lawns and ornamental trees and shrubs 156
12 Soil sterilisation, and warm-water treatment of plants 162
13 Formulae of insecticides and fungicides, and details of fumigants and dusts 164
14 Harmless and beneficial insects 170
15 Recognition 174

**List of
Illustrations**

Black and white photographs

Male cockchafer in flight	20
Cabbage root fly on cauliflower	38
Cabbage stem weevil maggots	40
Tomato root-knot eelworm	43
Chrysanthemum leaf miner	77
Lackey moth egg band	93
Winter moth caterpillars	95
Greasebanding fruit trees	96
Codlin moth caterpillar	97
Bud moth larva and Tortrix moth larvae	98
Apple sawfly damage	100
Magpie or currant moth larvae	108
Brown rot of apple	126
Scab on pears	144
Ladybird larva on rosebud	171
Caterpillar killed by parasitical larvae	175

Colour photographs

Cockchafer larva   *Facing page 64*
Cockchafer or 'May Bug', male
Common earwig, female
Crane-Fly or daddy-long-legs, female
Leatherjacket – larva of crane-fly   *Facing page 65*
Common millipede
Common centipede
Colorado beetle
White aphids on beech leaf   *Facing page 96*
Hover fly, female
Tomato moth
Violet ground beetle
Tomato moth caterpillar   *Facing page 97*
Adult Parasite (Encarsia formosa)
Parasite eating red spider mite
Whitefly scales unparasitised and parasitised

Preface

There always seems to have been the need for a book giving details of all the principal pests and diseases which the gardener is likely to come up against.

There are books on the pests and diseases of fruit trees. There are books on the diseases of vegetables. There is at least one book on the pests of greenhouse crops, but there seems to be no comprehensive modern work which deals in fair detail with the pests and diseases of fruits, vegetables, flowers, ornamental trees and shrubs as well as glasshouse crops.

When I was asked to write such a book I realised that I should have to consult the works of large numbers of authorities. I want frankly to acknowledge the great help that I have received in the past from numbers of eminent entomologists and mycologists who have helped me when a County Horticultural Adviser and when a Lecturer and Examiner to Horticultural Colleges.

We in this country owe much to the economic biologists who have worked silently and unobtrusively (in most cases) in order to find out not only the life history of a pest or disease, but also the best methods of control.

I would like to pay tribute here and now to such men as the late Dr A. M. Massee of the East Malling Research Station, the late Mr G. Fox Wilson of the Royal Horticultural Society and Dr H. Wormald, the late Assistant Director of the East Malling Research Station.

It is to men like these that a gardener like myself owes a debt of gratitude. Undoubtedly the good in this book is theirs and if errors should creep in they will be my own!

I should like to thank Miss Gweneth Wood, Dip. Hort. (Swanley), Mrs G. Ellis, Dip. Hort. (Midland), Miss G. Russell, Gold Medallist RHS, Miss E. Kerr, Dip. Hort. (Studley), and Miss M. Call, Dip. Hort. (Studley), all Technical Assistants of The International Horticultural Advisory Bureau, for all their help in making this book what it is today, while of course my thanks go also to Mrs Beryl Lovelock, my personal secretary who typed the script of the book very carefully.

W. E. SHEWELL-COOPER

1 The pest and disease problem examined

Presumably, ever since the time that Adam and Eve were turned out of the Garden of Eden, the gardener has had to cope with pests and diseases attacking his crops. These troubles have appeared to increase rather than decrease and this is probably because, in times of peace, we are very international in the exchange of plants.

The advent of the liner and aeroplane has brought countries far closer together and there is no doubt that pests have travelled on planes from one country to another. There are evidences, too, that diseases which were known, for instance, to exist only in Australasia have been transported to this country by some means and have proved specially troublesome here.

It is true that certain laws have been invoked in order to try and stem the movement of pests and diseases. There is a law, for instance, with regard to the Colorado beetle which arrived in Europe from America comparatively few years ago and which has spread with alarming rapidity from Spain to France, from France to Belgium, from Belgium to Germany, Germany to Switzerland and so on. It isn't possible to send plants either to Canada or America without certain certificates from the Ministry of Agriculture. Despite these restrictions, however, pests and diseases do spread. They may be carried on the legs of migratory birds. They may come over in packages from foreign countries. They may even be brought over on the fusilage of air liners or on the decks of tramp steamers – who knows!

There has been a tendency, too, for an increase in the pest and disease population of this country owing to a lack of knowledge in pathological control. In the old days the larger estates were well stocked with gardeners whose job it was to grow the best crops and to keep pests and diseases down. Small houses had little garden space. Nowadays all this is altered – nearly every house has a sizeable garden, but does the owner really bother about pests and disease control when he has got the garden? Too frequently the minimum of work is done in the garden and so the plot may become a breeding ground for all kinds of troubles. The large estates, on the other hand, are being broken up. Landowners cannot afford to keep 'the garden' as they did, and so there has been a decline in efficient pest control as a result.

Fortunately, all this time there has been a band of entomologists and mycologists who have been working out the best methods of pest and disease control year by year. It seems only a few years ago when no one knew how to keep down the Big Bud in blackcurrants, but now this pest is easy to control by the use of lime-sulphur. Slugs were a perpetual pest until the Draza remedy was introduced.

So the modern gardener has great advantages over the man who had to do similar work one hundred years ago. It isn't just a question of using lime and soot, as a kind of panacea for all ills. It is a question of having a garden medicine chest, as it were, which contains the right remedies and, once having recognised the disease or pest, the correct 'medicine' should be applied immediately.

Here is where too many amateur gardeners fail. First of all, they don't recognise the disease or pest until it is really serious and then, having recognised it, they haven't got the necessary remedy at hand. By the time this has been purchased the pest or disease has got a tremendous hold on the plant and it is almost impossible to control it as a result. Remedies, if they are to be effective, must be applied in the initial stages or even as a preventative before the pests and diseases are present.

CARE OF THE SOIL
The late Sir Albert Howard, who did so much to point out the importance of humus in the soil, states clearly in his book, *An Agricultural Testament*, that if the humus contents of the soil is built up then 'parasites' will disappear. He has demonstrated this in his own garden. It is, therefore, of the greatest importance to see, first of all, that soil is properly and regularly fed with organic matter. It is surely fatal to apply artificial fertilisers (chemical manures) continually without the use of farmyard manure, composted vegetable refuse, spent hops, or similar material. Under the guidance of its able Council, The Good Gardeners' Association (The International Association of Organic Gardeners) is doing all it can to make people 'humus conscious' as well as advising the use of compost only.

To put it simply – plants need feeding properly in exactly

the same way as human beings. When humans are ill nourished they are much more subject to diseases than when they are properly fed. See, therefore, that your ground is supplied with organic matter each year, and you will not have the same need to use insecticides and fungicides as you will have if you feed only with chemical fertilisers.

DIAGNOSIS

Half the battle of trying to cure a disease or kill a pest is being able to diagnose the trouble correctly. It is no use trying to kill a pest with poison which obtains its food by sucking the sap in the middle of the leaf. The only insects that you can kill with poison are those which actually eat the leaves and stems, like caterpillars.

Insects that suck have to be killed with a spray like nicotine or derris which paralyses their nerve centres.

The whole point of this book depends on the diagnoses, so do read the explanations very carefully and make certain before you apply a spray or a dust what the trouble really is. It is always worth while buying a magnifying glass or a little lens in order that a tiny pest may be seen more clearly or a disease brought out in relief.

Don't belong to the class of gardener who classifies all troubles as 'blight' or 'fly' and never tries to discriminate at all. Don't imitate the amateur who always uses one panacea for all ills as I have already said – that of soot and lime. Again and again I have been told – 'I applied soot and lime, but that didn't seem to stop it'.

Try to recognise the beginning stages of diseases and pests. Look out, for instance for the eggs of the moths, so as to be able to destroy them before they hatch out into caterpillars. Try and notice troubles such as Scab and Mildew when they first attack the leaves for, if you do, you can 'scotch' the trouble right at the beginning.

CORRECT APPLICATION

Having learnt to diagnose the troubles, learn to apply the remedies in the correct manner and at the right time. The old saying 'A stitch in time saves nine' is very true with plant diseases. There is usually one vulnerable stage in their life's history. Apply the cure then and all is over. Allow the vulnerable stage to pass and it may be impossible to save the plant.

Spraying or dusting before or after the critical period is useless. Therefore, follow the instructions given in this book exactly. A great deal of research has gone into finding out the best times for controlling all plant troubles.

Take a typical example – the Leaf Curling Aphids of plum or blackcurrant. If the trees and bushes are sprayed with a tar distillate wash in the winter, the eggs will be killed and there won't be any aphids to trouble the leaves in the spring. Once these pests get on to the lower surface of the leaves, they suck them and the leaves curl up, and it is then almost impossible to reach them with any kind of spray.

Be prepared to spray or dust at any time. Keep a sharp look out and don't waste a moment. That is why it is so important, as has already been said, to have a garden medicine chest with the remedies all ready.

SUITING THE REMEDY TO THE TROUBLE

Mention has already been made of the importance of applying the right remedy.

Generally speaking, all remedies may be divided into seven groups. (1) Fungicides (2) Fumigants and Smokes (3) Preventatives (4) Poison Baits (5) Corrosive Sprays (6) Stomach Poisons (7) Contact Paralysers. *Fungicides* These are used for killing fungus diseases, and fungus diseases may be called lowly little plants which live on the leaves, stems or bark of other plants. Typical fungicides are lime-sulphur (a brown liquid), Bordeaux Mixture and wettable sulphur and copper. There are also such dusts as sulphur and copper-lime. *Fumigants and Smokes* Fumigants can only be used, as a rule, in the greenhouse – though sometimes they are used in the soil. They are usually gases of one form or another, either applied as liquid or powder first and, as a result, gas is given off – or occasionally as definite gases in the first place.

'Smokes' are generated by 'burning' a special substance in a generator.

A common soil fumigant is carbon bi-sulphate, while fumigants in the greenhouse vary from naphthalene to nicotine, and from cyanogas to sulphur fumes. *Preventatives* These are used for preventing an insect or a fungus attacking a plant. Whizzed naphthalene may be applied along the rows of carrots, for instance, and the objectionable smell given off keeps the carrot fly away. Grease bands, when put round the fruit trees, prevent the females of winter moths (which are wingless) from crawling up the trunks and laying their eggs in the branches. Whenever possible, preventative measures are detailed throughout the book. *Poison Baits* It is sometimes possible to place baits in the vicinity of plants that are likely to be attacked by a pest and so lure the insects away to their death. These poison baits, for instance, are very useful in the case of slugs, where a mixture of bran and metaldehyde lures these pests quickly to their doom. Poison baits are also also used for pests like wasps which are apt to attack ripe fruit in the summer. Jars of syrupy material are hung up in the trees to which a little poison has been added. *Corrosive Sprays* (for those who do not mind using them) Corrosive sprays are usually used in the winter, especially in the case of fruit trees. These have a slight burning action and so destroy the eggs of insects as well as any other actual pests which may still be lurking about. It is impossible to use corrosive sprays in the summer, for though the pests would be killed, the leaves of course would be burned. *Stomach Poisons.* In this case the spray or dust used – and it is usually a spray – deposits a film of poison all over the leaf and, in consequence, any insect pest which eats the leaf is poisoned. It is perhaps the cheapest form of pest control known. It is usually against caterpillars and beetles and some weevils. *Contact Paralysers.* The only way to kill insects which suck – like aphids and the apple sucker – in the summer is to paralyse them by applying a wash like nicotine or liquid derris. It is no good trying to kill them with stomach poisons.

But, in addition, substances like nicotine and liquid derris will kill other pests such as caterpillars, for their nerve centres will be paralysed also. Many people look upon a liquid derris wash as a kind of standard wash for this reason, and use it throughout the summer as a 'panacea'. Its great advantage is that it is not poisonous to human beings so there is no fear of killing young children. Nor does it cause the deaths of family pets.

SOFT WATER BETTER THAN HARD

It is always better to use soft water rather than hard water when making up sprays. Rain water is most suitable for it contains hardly any mineral matter. Sea or brackish waters are quite unsuitable, while water from the tap may or may not be too hard. It will depend largely on the district. Those who have water softeners installed are very fortunate.

PREDATORS

The use of predators and parasites is extremely important and details will be found in chapters 14 and 15.

2   Hygiene in the garden

PREVENTION BETTER THAN CURE

In the garden much can be done to prevent the attacks of pests
and diseases if every care is taken to destroy the breeding-
grounds. One of the commonest places for the hibernation of
insects is in the rubbish of hedge bottoms. It is necessary,
therefore, to clean out all hedge bottoms regularly and to
compost the rubbish thus obtained.

Weeds should never be allowed to develop anywhere for
these often prove alternative food or hosts to the diseases or
pests. Mulching with compost or sedge peat will prevent
weeds appearing and will provide the nourishment that plants
so much appreciate.

There should be no dirty corners in a garden. Sometimes
you walk round a garden and find everything looking neat and
tidy, and then you ask to see the rubbish heap, or the place
where the bonfire is made, and you find here the most awful
untidiness, heaps of this, and heaps of that, old boxes, old pots
and so on, all lying about untidily, providing as a result,
breeding-grounds for the many troubles which afflict the gardener.

COMPOSTING

It is most important, therefore, to see that the whole garden is
tidied up, and that there are no nooks or crannies where plant
enemies may lurk. Rubbish heaps should be done away with
and compost heaps should take their place. These should be
neat and tidy and the material put thereon should be rotted
down by the use of an active fish manure, poultry manure or
seaweed manure.

Any of these should be applied at the rate of 3 oz to the sq.
yd for every 6 in. thickness of vegetable refuse collected. Every
now and then a fork may be plunged into the heap and be
stirred about slightly so as to let in air, and should the weather
be very dry, such a heap should be given a thorough watering.

DEAD AND DISEASED MATERIAL

Dead wood should never be allowed to remain in trees. It should be removed immediately it is seen. Badly diseased branches should be sawn off also.

The same thing applies to other plants. Always remove leaves that are diseased and, in bad cases, take up whole plants and see that they are composted. It is advisable, too, to remove the weakly plants for they are much more likely to be attacked by enemies than those which are sturdy and strong.

The bonfire should be used only for burning the diseased wood. Bonfires are useful in that they provide wood ash and this is valuable potash for the soil. Don't leave the branches of fruit trees lying about until you have time to make a bonfire, for all this time the breeding of pests and diseases may be going on and the trouble getting worse and worse. If material has to be burnt because it is diseased – burn it immediately.

CORRECT FEEDING

Much can be done to see that plants grow robust and strong if they are properly fed. The soil should be enriched year after year with properly made compost and, in addition, it may be necessary to give a fish manure or meat and bonemeal at 3 oz to the sq. yd. The use of too much nitrogen is often the cause of soft plants, such plants being liable to both fungus diseases and insect pest attacks.

This isn't the time or place to go into full details of manures and manuring, but these will be found in other books of mine such as *The Basic Book of Vegetable Growing*.

ROOM FOR DEVELOPMENT

In too many cases, gardeners do not give plants sufficient room for development and when plants are crowded together they suffer naturally from diseases. Brussels sprouts which should be planted 3 ft square are often put in 2 ft by 18 in. and then people wonder why they are badly attacked by the 'blue bug' or by mildew.

Fruit trees and bushes, rose trees, ornamental plants as well as vegetables all need light and air, and where a gardener takes the trouble to thin his plants early and to space them out well, he never has to spend so much money on insecticides and fungicides.

EFFICIENT DRAINAGE

It is impossible for trees and plants to grow properly if their roots are standing in water the whole time, or even if their 'feet' are deep in water all the winter and then are dried out in the summer.

Some method of draining the excess moisture away must be arranged. On the farm and market garden this is done by agricultural land drains and these are often quite a possibility in an ordinary garden.

WATER SUPPLY

It is just as important to have sufficient moisture present in the soil as it is to ensure that the roots are not drowned. Plants that are suffering from drought are often badly attacked by both pests and diseases. The gardener should therefore try to see (1) that sufficient organic matter is put on top of the soil to act as a mulch and hold the moisture, (2) try if possible to have an overhead sprinkling apparatus so that thorough waterings can be given by means of a hose plus this whirling Rain Sprinkler during dry periods.

THE USE OF LIME

Soil acidity is often a cause of trouble. Fortunately this can be corrected by an application of lime and most gardeners find garden lime convenient for this purpose. It should be applied as a top dressing at, say, 5 – 6 oz per sq. yd in February. Lime definitely helps to keep down the Club Root disease and it also releases plant foods which help to keep the right balance in the soil.

The exact amount of lime which should be used can always be determined in a few minutes by the use of a BDH Soil Indicator. These can be purchased at any good chemist for a reasonable sum. Readers who care to join the International Association of Organic Gardeners can have their soil tested for lime gratis. Write to the Association (which is also called the Good Gardeners' Association) at Arkley Manor, Arkley, S. Herts. for particulars, enclosing a s.a.e. for a reply.

3 Pests that attack plants generally

There are a large number of insect pests which attack all kinds of plants. In order to save repetition, therefore, these will be included in this chapter under their own common names and placed for convenience in alphabetical order.

If it is necessary, for some reason or other, to mention one of the pests specifically in another chapter as well, a note will be found at suitable points connecting the two references.

ANTS

Ants swarm over plants which are infested with aphids (greenfly) which they seek for the sake of the sweet excretion, the so-called Honeydew. Some species of ants even transfer aphids from one plant to another and in glasshouses some transport Mealy Bugs.

Ants are responsible for the death of many plants in rock gardens, herbaceous borders and in glasshouses for they form their nests among the plants, and the roots, thus being loosened from the soil, wilt and die. *Control Measures* The most satisfactory method of control is to find the ants' nests, make a hole in the centre of each and to pour into it about $\frac{1}{2}$ fl. oz carbon bi-sulphide – a highly inflammable liquid – or a solution of sodium cyanide – a poisonous substance – and then to tread firmly to conserve the fumes.

Ants' nests in garden paths may be destroyed by watering with a weed-killer or by pouring boiling water, petrol or paraffin into the holes. Liquid derris may be used neat.

'Nippon' is an excellent Japanese remedy. It kills ants, but is non-poisonous to all animals and humans. It is harmless to all plant life, odourless and can therefore be applied with safety, even in the larder. The ants vanish completely to die in their nest.

APHIDS (Many species)
Sometimes called Greenflies, Blueflies, Blackfly, Plant Lice and so on. Biological name Aphis (pl. Aphides).

Probably the best known and most persistent of all plant pests, both in the open and under glass. There is hardly a plant they won't attack.

Many of the species of aphids have complicated life-stories. They often migrate from cultivated plants to weeds, back to secondary host-plants, and so on. They may attack in the spring, leave in the summer and then come back again in the late summer.

Not only do they suck the sap, distort the foliage, ruin flowers and check growth, but they also help to transmit diseases like canker in apples and various viruses like the Lily Mosaic.

They usually deposit on the leaves and stems of plants an excretion known as 'Honeydew' which the ants lick. If the aphids are controlled, therefore, the ants will be kept away also. *Control Measures* In the winter – if you have no objection to tar oil – fruit trees and bushes, deciduous ornamental trees and shrubs can be sprayed with a tar distillate wash in order to kill the eggs and over-wintering females. Dissolving 1 pt of an efficient tar oil in 10 pts of water is necessary in bad cases; though 1 in 20 is often sufficient.

In the spring and summer it is necessary to spray plants with an insecticide which will paralyse them and kill them. The spray must be applied with force, to hit the under-surface of the leaves as well as the upper surface and to cover the whole of the plant concerned.

The best washes used are: (a) nicotine and soft soap (for formula, see chapter 13). (b) derris. There are various proprietary preparations which should be used according to the instructions found on the tin or bottle. Liquid derris gives good results. (c) Dusting with nicotine dust or derris dust. It is, however, always better to spray, if possible. Pyrethrum added to derris makes for better control in bad cases.

Under glass it is, of course, possible to fumigate or to use a 'smoke' and special instructions on the subject will be found in chapter 13. A good fumigant consists of $\frac{1}{6}$ fl. oz pure nicotine plus $\frac{1}{6}$ fl. oz methylated spirit to each 1,000 cu. ft of greenhouse space inside. This should be vaporised in a small tin placed over a spirit lamp.

Keep down all weeds in the vicinity of the garden or allotment. On these the aphids may breed.

Grease-bands placed on trees will prevent ants from climbing the trunks and either distributing or hunting aphids.

CHAFER BEETLES (*Melolontha vulgaris*, *Phyllopertha horticola*, *Cetonia aurata*)

For the purpose of this book, the cock-chafer, garden-chafer and rose-chafer (the Latin names of which are found above in this order) will be treated as one for the control measures are almost the same.

The cock-chafers will be seen flying in the evening. During the day they are still. The female lays 70 or more eggs which hatch out in 6 weeks time into thick greyish-white grubs which live in the ground for 2 or 3 summers. These are $1\frac{1}{2}$ in. long and have three pairs of legs. They attack the roots of perennial plants.

Male cock-chafer in flight—taken by electronic flash.

The summer-chafer appears in June and July, being two-thirds of an inch long. It is similar to the cock-chafer in appearance. The grubs do similar damage.

Garden-chafers are only $\frac{1}{2}$ in. long, the front part of the body being of a metallic lustre, and the wing cases being brownish red. The beetles eat the leaves of plants and may do a great deal of harm.

The green rose-chafer is beautiful, being golden green, the wing cases being covered with white spots. They appear in May and June and are very harmful to flowers. *Control Measures* Fork in whizzed napthalene at 1 oz to the sq. yd in the autumn and again early in the spring. This will help to eliminate the damage done by the grubs. Compost, by encouraging birds to scratch has a good control of chafer bugs.

Spray the plants attacked by the beetles with arsenate of lead, using a spreader. For details as to make-up, see chapter 13.

Adult beetles can be controlled by dusting or spraying the foliage and stems with Pyrethrum, but the grubs are less easily controlled.

CATERPILLARS   See Surface Caterpillars below.

EARWIGS (*Forficula auricularia*)
Some authorities say that earwigs do little harm, while others state that they can cause great havoc by feeding on the foliage and blooms of plants. Though they do attack large numbers of different kinds of plants, they seem principally to infest chrysanthemums, dahlias and sweet peas.

Where, however, they are found in large numbers in any garden, they should be destroyed.

In the spring, the female lays her eggs in a hole she makes in the earth, usually below stones. She lays about 30 eggs in each cache, and watches them hatch out into a small earwig-like white insect. The mother earwig then dies and the young ones feed on her body, departing afterwards to go their own ways. They can usually be found fully grown early in June, and they are often a serious pest from the month of August onwards.   *Control Measures*   If the pest becomes very bad, the affected plants may be sprayed with nicotine and soft soap (for formula see chapter 13).

All dead and curled-up leaves should be picked off from the base of plants and flower-pots stuffed with straw, hay or wood wool should be inverted on bamboos and stood among the plants normally attacked. Every morning each pot should be removed and the earwigs present should be shaken out into a tin of paraffin.

Use pyrethrum dust on plants likely to be infested. Indoor chrysanthemums should be dusted as soon as they are brought into the greenhouse. The pyrethrum will also be effective against Chrysanthemum Leaf Miner at the same time.

EELWORMS (Various)

There are a very large number of different kinds and types of eelworms which attack the vegetables and flowering plants of a garden. Plants commonly attacked are potato, tomato, chrysanthemum, phlox, Sweet William, iris, tulip and narcissus.

Eelworms are minute and are usually invisible to the naked eye. As their name suggests, they are eel-shaped, the body tapering slightly towards the head and sharply to a pointed tail.

Eelworms are colourless, slender and microscopic, the adults being no more than 1 mm. long. After mating, each female usually lays 25–35 eggs. The estimated length of the life cycle from egg to egg is 10–14 days. The life-cycle varies from plant to plant but the eggs are usually laid somewhere in the plant tissues and the larvae which hatch out resemble their parents.

The same species of eelworm can infest the leaves of a number of other plants, e.g. aster, calceolaria, delphinium, doronicum, peony, phlox, pyrethrum, Saintpaulia, verbena and zinnia. It is also a common pest of strawberries and blackcurrant. It can live successfully on various common weeds such as buttercup, chickweed, goosegrass, groundsel, sowthistle and speedwell; hence the importance of weed control after removal of infested crops.

In the case of phlox, Sweet William and chrysanthemum, the eelworm swims up the film of moisture around the stems and enters the leaves by the breathing pores. Here they distort the leaf, often causing it to turn brown. The stems may be stunted and split or they may be elongated and whippy.

In the case of bulbs, the eelworms usually enter through the tip and live in the bulb, breeding for long periods. Bulbs thus attacked produce only short foliage and small flowers on short stems; if they flower at all. The bulbs usually become soft, especially when the attack is far advanced.

The eelworms which attack potatoes cause the plants to become stunted and produce poor crops. If the roots are examined, little nodules or cysts will be found on them, these being called 'Root Knots' which gives the pest its particular name of Root Knot Eelworm. *Control Measures* In the case of narcissus bulbs the best method of control is by the use of the warm-water bath (see chapter 12).

With chrysanthemums, the roots should be treated with a hot water bath at 110°F for 20 minutes just before they are put out in the frames or in boxes to grow cuttings. Another method is to immerse the cuttings in warm water at 110°F. for 20 minutes and to strike these in eelworm-free soil.

With phlox, control may be obtained if cuttings are taken from washed roots only, for the eelworms live in the stems and leaves and not in the roots.

Other important methods of control are:

(1) Regular hoeing to eliminate weeds
(2) The burning of diseased stems and *not* placing them on rubbish heaps.
(3) The carrying out of a rotation of crops in order that susceptible types are not grown on the same piece of ground year after year.
(4) Sterilising with steam or boiling water of boxes and frames and, where possible, soil.

The Phlox eelworm will attack enothera badly.

The Chrysanthemum Eelworm will attack dahlia, delphinium, rudbeckia, aster and verbena venosa, etc., *Natural Control* At the research gardens of The Good Gardeners' Association, it has been shown that there beneficial fungi in compost which actually eat the Chrysanthemum eelworms. Thus, by applying properly made compost one can guarantee that any eelworms present will be killed naturally by fungal predators. *Reinfestation* If infected plants, or other sources of infection are brought into the house after jection has been carried out, reinfestation may easily occur, though this will be a slow process. Seed and potting composts should therefore be sterilised.

LEATHER JACKETS (*Tipula oleracea, etc.*)
Leather jackets are the larvae of the crane-fly or daddy-longlegs. In the north they are sometimes called the 'bots'.

They like damp conditions and they often die in the ground in drought.

They feed on all parts of plants growing underground such as roots, tubers and corms, tunnelling into and eating them. They can do great harm to lawns, vegetables, flowers and to herbaceous borders. They feed throughout the winter when conditions are favourable and, as the result of their damage, they may let in millipedes and fungus organisms.

They are usually $1 - 1\frac{1}{2}$ in. long, of a greyish-brown or blackish colour, are legless and have a tough, leathery skin.

The eggs are laid by the crane-flies in late August and early September, a single female being able to deposit 300. In 14 days the larvae hatch out and start to feed on the roots of plants, going on doing so through the autumn, winter and the following spring. *Control Measures* See that the soil is properly drained; hoe regularly throughout the spring and summer as continual soil disturbance proves distasteful to the larvae.

Fork into the ground whizzed napthalene, at the rate of 3 oz to the sq. yd, and if dry, water afterwards.

MILLIPEDES (*Blanjulus guttulatus* and *Polydesmus complanatus*)
Millipedes must be distinguished from centipedes, for the former are harmful and the latter are beneficial. Millipedes, when disturbed, curl themselves up. They are slow to move and have two pairs of legs, to almost all their body segments. Their bodies are rounded and usually darkish in colour.

Centipedes, on the other hand, usually run away when disturbed, being active. Their bodies are flattened and they only have one pair of legs to each segment.

Millipedes feed on vegetable matter, both dead and living – both in the open and under glass. They will attack the baby leaves of seedlings. They will gnaw the underground stems and roots of plants. They will burrow into bulbs, corms and tubers and they will eat seeds. They often follow on the damage caused by other pests such as wire worms or slugs.

They make an entry for the invasion of fungus diseases and bacterial organisms.

The breeding takes place in the late spring and summer, the female laying her eggs inside a sealed-up nest low down in the soil; the eggs hatch out in 10 days. *Control Measures* Whizzed napthalene may be forked in at 3 oz to the square yd. Incorporate this in the top 8 in. of soil and it will act as a repellent for 2 or 3 months.

Hoe regularly for this pest dislikes surface soil movement.

Trap by means of scooped-out potato, turnip or swede skewered on to a length of bamboo, and pull up and look at every 3 or 4 days. Drop the pests found into a small tin of paraffin.

See that all soils are properly drained and give the surface of the ground a heavy dressing of lime at, say, $\frac{1}{2}$ lb. to the sq. yd.

Mustard Sow Mustard seed at $\frac{1}{2}$ lb. to the sq. yd in the spring or summer. When the plants are 6 in. high, cut them down. Dust them and the area with fish manure at 3 oz to the sq. yd and fork in lightly. Such treatment invariably eliminates the wireworms.

SLUGS AND SNAILS
There are, unfortunately, many different kinds of slugs and snails, some of which are more numerous than others. The slugs may be classified as follows:
(1) The Large Black Slug, which is less commonly injurious to plants but sometimes causes damage.
(2) The Garden Slug, a small dark species with a yellow foot and a very tough skin, common both in gardens and fields.
(3) The White-soled Slug, also a small species, generally grey in colour with a flattened appearance and with a strikingly white foot.
(4) The Field Slug, variable in colour but usually mottled grey with a reddish or yellow tinge; it is probably the most uniformly and generally injurious slug throughout the country.
(5) The Keeled Slug, dark brown or grey with body keeled along the back. A very troublesome species. Largely subterranean in habit, feeding on the underground parts of plants and often specially injurious to potatoes.
    The snails are:
(1) The Large Garden Snail, the most common and widely distributed species of snail, easily distinguishable by the large grey-brown shell with paler markings.
(2) The Banded Snail, more injurious to farm crops than to garden crops as a whole. The shell may be white, grey, pale yellow, pink or brown with one to five spiral darker bands.

Generally speaking, slugs and snails are night marauders and eat anything fresh and green and succulent. Some seem to prefer roots and tubers and so attack below ground – others go for the parts of the plant above ground level. Slugs will burrow deep down during the winter in order to escape the frost.

Snails, on the other hand, collect in large numbers, as a rule in a dry sheltered place.

Slugs usually prefer a soil rich in moisture – the heavy soils and clays. They also congregate in decayed vegetable matter. *Natural enemies* Birds eat them greedily, especially rooks, starlings and blackbirds. Ducks love them, and some people allow their Khaki Campbells or Indian Runners to roam the vegetable garden in the winter when there are few crops to harm. Toads and moles eat slugs, whilst snails are devoured by thrushes. *Control Measures* (1) Hand picking. Place used orange or grapefruit skins upside down on the soil, pick up the slugs that collect under them and place them in paraffin.

(2) Copper sulphate and lime method. Use powdered copper sulphate and garden lime, mixed together in equal parts. Fork this mixture in lightly, using 1 oz per sq. yd or even a slightly heavier dressing than this. A second similar dressing may be worked in 15 days before sowing seeds or setting out plants. The danger, of course, is the copper sulphate which, if overdone, may poison the soil.

(3) The Draza method. A blue granular bait that never fails under almost all conditions is sprinkled lightly all over the area concerned.

Amount to use For the average size garden use the blue granules at 4–5 oz to the sq. yd. In the glasshouse place the blue granules bait in tin lids or saucers on and below the staging.

General advice The granules should not be scattered over plants intended for human consumption such as vegetables, salads, strawberries and the like.

Draza bait is strongly attractive to slugs and snails but not to birds or animals and has a rapid initial action, killing off the pests quickly.

(4) The barrier method. Some of the copper sulphate and hydrated lime mixture or metaldehyde bait may be used from time to time along the edge of gardens or allotments to prevent the passage of slugs onto one's own particular portion of ground. The barriers will, however, be washed away by heavy rains and must then be renewed.

(5) The true organic growers need have no trouble with slugs. The powdery compost applied all over the soil to the depth of an inch makes the movement of slugs impossible and they die.

When proper compost is not available medium sedge peat can be used instead.

SURFACE CATERPILLARS, Cut Worms (*Euxoa segetum, E. exclamationis, Graphiphora pronuba*)

These pests feed at night on the underground parts of plants, on the lower leaves and on the the stems. They often nibble a plant just above or below ground level. The result is that such a plant will snap off or wilt.

During the day they hide away under the surface of the soil and under leaves and stems.

The caterpillars are either a dirty grey with blackish dots on their sides or yellowish greenish-grey, having black or greenish stripes along the sides of their bodies.

The first damage is usually seen in August but the trouble continues throughout the autumn and winter.

They are usually full grown and pupate any time during the months of February, March and April. *Control Measures* In the case of small outbreaks, look for the caterpillars after dark with the aid of an electric torch. Look especially for them in the vicinity of wilting plants. Hoe regularly between all plants.

As cutworms work after dark, pyrethrum or derris dust sprinkled around their haunts will destroy them.

THRIPS (*Heliothrips haemorrhoidalis*, Common thrip, *Thrips tabaci* Tobacco thrip)

On the whole, thrips are far more common under glass than they are in the open, but they do attack a great number of plants causing, in the case of flowers, distortion of the blooms and mottling of the leaves and, in the case of peas and beans, they attack the stems, leaves and pods, causing the latter to look silver in the early stages and later turn brown.

The adult thrips are slender and elongated. They are seldom a tenth of an inch in length and they may be black, brown or yellow in colour. They lay their eggs in the leaves, pushing these eggs below the leaf surface with a special egg-laying apparatus. Small transparent insects hatch out and feed on the leaves and, where they feed, white areas are seen, surrounded by little black dots – their excreta.

The adults which fly get into sheltered places throughout the winter and, in the hot summer conditions, many generations are produced in a short space of time. In the greenhouse these insects breed continuously.

Outside they may attack seedlings, sucking the sap from their growing points and thus distorting the plants, and preventing them from growing healthily. They are worse in a dry season than in a rainy period.

A simple method of telling whether a plant is attacked by thrips or not is to hold a clean white handkerchief close to the plant and then watch to see whether, on tapping the plant sharply, tiny little black specks drop on to the material. These little black specks will be found to wriggle and, if examined with a magnifying glass, will be seen to be of the shape already described. *Control Measures* Keep plants growing healthily by seeing that the soil receives sufficient moisture, by not overcrowding and by not allowing them to suffer from draught. Syringing regularly with clear water helps to kill the insects for it washes them off the leaves on the the soil where they die of starvation.

Spraying with nicotine, using $\frac{3}{4}$ oz to 10 gal. water, plus a spreader three times at weekly intervals has proved very effective. By this method the eggs within a leaf have the opportunity of hatching out and the third spraying catches the remainder of the population.

In the greenhouse fumigation with nicotine vapour is usually effective if carried out once a week for three weeks. In the case, however, of carnation, cyclamen and arum, grade 16 naphthalene should be sprinkled along the paths at the rate of 10 oz per 1,000 cu. ft.

WIREWORMS (*Agriotes lineatus, Agricotes obscurus* and *Athous haemorrhoidalis*)

The wireworm is the larvae of the Click Beetle and is perhaps the most widely distributed of all the soil pests. The click beetle or skip-jack as it is sometimes called is brown in colour and possesses the faculty of being able to bend the fore part of the body away from the hind part, suddenly straightening itself again with a clicking sound. In this way it can jump vertically into the air, and when placed on its back can easily right itself.

The click beetle will be seen flying about in the sun during the months of May and June. The eggs are laid in grass, either singly or in clusters, during the months of June and July but occasionally eggs can be found in cultivated land. The larvae, which hatch out in a month, feed on the roots of the grass or on decaying vegetable matter, and it is only when they are a year old that they really begin to feed on the underground portions of all kinds of plants. Unfortunately, they continue to remain and feed in the soil for four or five years before turning into beetles again. They can during this time do a great deal of damage and, as they live underground, they are extremely difficult to poison.

Their main feeding periods appear to be the spring and autumn though, in some years, they continue feeding right the way through the season. During the winter – so it has been found – the wireworms burrow lower into the soil so as to avoid being frozen, and then they come up to the surface again in the spring when the young plants are growing and are susceptible to injury.

Wireworms may be distinguished from millipedes and centipedes by the number of legs. A wireworm has only three pairs of short legs situated on the first three segments of its body. Millipedes and centipedes have legs all down their bodies. Wireworms, too, as their name implies, are very wiry, and difficult to kill by squeezing between the fingers. *Control Measures* Great care should be taken when purchasing turf for greenhouses or frames, for wireworms may be introduced in this and so start the trouble. Before buying turf two or three of the sods should be pulled to pieces to see whether any pests are visible.

Newly broken grassland which is infested can be 'cleaned' in one year by growing a potato crop which should be lifted in late summer and the wireworm riddled tubers fed to chickens, ducks or geese.

Sowing mustard on infested ground, thickly, has also proved useful. This should be forked in when about 18 in. high.

Naphthalene may be applied at 3–4 oz to the sq. yd and proves a deterrent to this pest. It doesn't actually kill, but it drives them away.

It is possible to trap wireworms by spitting pieces of carrot or potato on the end of a stick and burying these 2 in. deep in the ground. These traps should be removed at weekly intervals and the wireworms picked out and placed in a tin of paraffin.

Make holes in infested ground with a crowbar or walking stick 2 ft apart and 8–9 in. deep, and drop into the bottom of each hole a piece of para-dichlor-benzene, the size of a French bean. Tread down the holes immediately afterwards. The chemical volatilises through the soil, killing the wireworms. It is possible to make the holes in between rows of crops in the spring and early summer, or on vacant ground in the autumn or winter. If it is used in the summer between root crops or potatoes it may cause them to be tainted. Rotovating virgin ground 2–3 in. deep before planting is quite effective.

WOODLICE

Sometimes called Pea-bugs, Pill-bugs, Sow-bugs etc. They are abundant in town gardens and prefer shady situations and decaying organic matter to live in. They hide away in the day time in crevices beneath stones, in brickwork, in decaying stumps of trees, under boards and wooden edgings of paths and under heaps of leaves. They live chiefly on decaying vegetable matter but often attack living plants, gnawing and devouring the stems. They will eat out irregular holes in the leaves of a large number of plants under glass and in the open.

Young woodlice are delicate looking and whitish. *Control Measures* Spray with liquid pyrethrum or dust with pyrethrum powder after dark when the creatures are moving over soil surface. Place scooped-out potato tubers or turnip roots upside down on surface soil. The creatures will hide in these and may then be collected.

4 Diseases that attack plants generally

CLUB ROOT

This disease is often known as 'Finger-and-toe' or 'Anbury' and will attack the roots of any member of the family *Cruciferae*, i.e. cabbage, caluliflower, turnip, radish, wallflower, stock and some weeds like charlock and shepherd's purse.

The roots of affected plants swell and become knotted and distorted. When broken open these swellings are found to contain rotten, evil-smelling material. The plants are dwarf, they look sickly, and never really come to anything. *Control Measures* First of all, clean healthy plants must be raised.

For thirty years the author had no difficulty at all in controlling Club Root, but during the last five years or so the good old remedy has failed, so, at the moment of publishing this book, several ideas are being fairly successfully tried out.

It is obvious that the plasmodium that causes the trouble has become more and more virile. It is attracted by the smell of cabbage roots and soon 'swims over' and enters a root hair and soon starts its nefarious work.

In order to prevent the plasmodium 'smelling' the Brassica root, it is possible to pour boiling water into the hole at planting time and this, it has been observed, gives the roots – as it were – 'a flying start.

A second method found to be quite successful in some gardens is to cut a garlic clove into two and to put one section into the hole made by the dibber or trowel at the time of planting. The strong sulphur smell of the garlic keeps the disease organism at bay.

VERTICILLIUM WILT (*Verticillium albo-atrum*)

This disease occurs on many herbaceous as well as ornamental plants, and causes them to wither in the middle of perfect growth. When the stems are cut through the wood vessels appear dark green or brown in colour. The fungus over-winters in the soil on diseased plant tissues, or in tubers of such plants as dahlia, and can be disseminated by means of the cuttings. Aster, chrysanthemum, dahlia, antirrhinum, lupin, poppy, carnation and paeonie may all be attacked by this disease. *Control Measures* Plants attacked should be removed and burnt. Susceptible plants should not be grown on infected areas for several years. Propagate from healthy stock. Dazomet soil fumigant, lightly forked in and watered to cap the soil will control this disease well, it completely breaks down after two months and leaves no ill effect.

SPOTTED WILT

This is a virus disease. It is usually transmitted from plant to plant by means of insects and may be recognised by the concentric ring, sometimes yellow and sometimes white, on the leaves, or a marking similar to that of 'Streak'. In very young plants the virus may cause them to die. If plants show any mottling when examined, and rings of a darker or lighter colour are seen, the presence of Spotted Wilt should be suspected. Even if the plants are not growing satisfactorily and no such rings are seen, Spotted Wilt may still be suspected.

The principal plants attacked are tomato, cucumber, melon, climbing French bean, aster, chrysanthemum, dahlia, zinnia. While working amongst plants it is possible to carry the disease from plant to plant by hand. *Control Measures* As this disease is so serious, directly it is suspected the attack should be confirmed by consulting immediately a recognised Horticultural Adviser.

Badly affected plants should be burnt at once and weeds such as the common plantain which can act as a host-plant, should be rigorously kept down.

Keep down all the pests that may be the cause of carrying infection, particularly aphides (greenfly), capsid bugs (tarnished plant bugs), thrips and the like.

THE VIRUS PROBLEM

Spotted Wilt, mentioned above, is a virus disease but it is so serious that it has purposely been placed under a separate heading. There are many other virus diseases, such as Yellow Edge and Crinkle in strawberry, Reversion in blackcurrant, Mosaic in raspberry, Yellow Stripe in narcissus, Stripe in Iris, and Break in tulip. These are dealt with in some detail under the individual plants themselves.

It is very difficult to explain exactly what a virus disease is. It may, however, be said to be an infection present in the plant juice. Dr Kenneth Smith in his book *Beyond the Microscope* says, 'The symptoms of the diseases they cause are almost the only way we have to know that viruses exist at all. They may therefore be what are called "obligate parasites", which means that they are incapable of existing independently.' Latterly he has been treating the viruses like organisms and more like chemical substances. Dr W. M. Stanley of the USA actually succeeded in isolating the virus from a diseased tobacco plant, the final result being an unusual protein which crystallised into long thin needles. At the present time it does seem as if viruses must be looked upon as a kind of chain connecting such 'things' as bacteria with chemicals.

Virus infection spreads extraordinarily quickly from plant to plant. It is for this reason that it is so important to burn badly infected plants so as to prevent the disease from being transmitted.

It is equally important to keep down pests, particularly sucking insects such as aphids and, in the case of blackcurrant, the big bud mite. The incidence of virus diseases is undoubtedly one of the most serious problems that faces the gardener today.

The infection sometimes causes dwarfing, sometimes distortion, sometimes definite streaking, sometimes tipping of the foliage and stems and sometimes blotching of the flowers and foliage. *Control Measures* No cure is known. The only thing to do is to (1) start with virus-free material; (2) keep down the pests already mentioned and (3) destroy affected plants.

It is possible today to obtain certified virus-free strawberries, virus-free raspberry canes, virus-free blackcurrants and so on. See also viruses under **Lettuce, Potato** and **Cucumber.**

5   The pests of vegetables

In chapter 3 details are given of pests that attack many
vegetables. Care should be taken, therefore, to study this
chapter first. No excuse is made for emphasising this point.
This chapter deals with the principal pests that attack
vegetables, together with the best methods of control. In some
cases reference is made to other pests.

Asparagus

ASPARAGUS BEETLE (*Crioceris asparagi*)
The asparagus beetle has a black head, black and yellow wing
cases, but the second portion of its body is bright red. It is,
therefore, quite easy to recognise. It is usually $\frac{1}{5}-\frac{1}{4}$ in. in length.
It lays its eggs from June onwards, first on the asparagus
shoots and later on the foliage after it has developed. The eggs
are spindle shaped, oval, greenish-brown in colour and are
fixed by their ends to the plants. They usually occur in rows of
3 to 5.

The eggs hatch out in five or seven days, into a grub half an
inch long, usually slate-coloured but sometimes almost yellow.
This grub feeds on the asparagus plant as does the beetle, and
disfigures the shoots and stems.

In very bad attacks the shoots become defiled and useless
from the masses of eggs and because of the sticky fluid emitted
by the grubs.

The beetles spend the winter hiding among any rubbish
that will give shelter. From the spring onwards, there may be
two or three generations in one year. *Control Measures* Keep the
beds dusted regularly with a good nicotine dust or use a
pyrethrum spray in order to kill the larvae and the beetles.
When the foliage is cut down in the autumn, collect it carefully
and burn it in order to destroy both beetles and grubs.

Leave small portions of a bed uncut to act as a trap crop.
The insects thus disturbed during the original cutting congregate on the stems that are left and may there be destroyed
by nicotine spraying.

Bean, Broad

BLACK APHIS OR BEAN APHIS (*Aphis rumicis*)
The black aphis – commonly known as the Black Blight, or Black Dolphin – large clusters of which form at the tops of broad bean plants and increase at such a rate that the shoots become covered with fly and with a sticky excrement.

During the winter the black aphis may be found on the shrub *Euonymus europaeus* (the spindle tree) in the egg stage. These eggs hatch out sometime during the month of March and the females then fly to the beans where they multiply exceedingly. *Control Measures* Any *eunonymus* trees in the garden should be sprayed with a strong Pyrethrum wash in the winter. It is well worthwhile spraying neighbours' trees and bushes with a similar wash if they will give permission for this to be done. Those who do not wish to spray should grub up the bushes and burn them together with any other spindle trees in the vicinity.

This aphis may over-winter on old mangolds and on sheltered self-sown plants. It is more difficult, therefore, to ensure winter control in the country than it is in the town.

On the broad beans themselves, spray with liquid derris when the blackfly is first seen. Other pests that attack broad beans are Thrips, Weevils and Beetles. (See **Pea**).

Bean Runner

RED SPIDER MITE (*Tetranychus telarius*)
Runner beans may be badly attacked with red spider mites in the summer. The attacks are usually particularly bad during drought years and it is then that control measures are necessary.

The leaves turn a brownish shade and if the underside is examined it will be found to be covered with minute white webs and, if a magnifying glass is used, the yellowish-red mites will be distinguished. *Control measures* It is always worthwhile, in gardens, to spray runner beans with clean water both in the evening and morning. The spraying should be done with as great a force as possible under the leaves.

Where it is impossible to syringe regularly, the plants may be sprayed with liver of sulphur, using 1 oz liver of sulphur to 8 gal. water. Stir in, in addition, a little soft soap. Use wettable sulphur if liver of sulphur is not available.

Other pests that may attack runner beans are Black Aphis (See **Bean Broad**).

Beetroot

MANGOLD FLY (*Pegomyia betae*)
This fly is very similar in appearance to the ordinary house-fly. It may be seen flying around the rows of beetroot or settling on the leaves. It lays its eggs in small groups on the underside of leaves, and the larvae tunnel in the same manner as the celery fly, causing blisters to appear. As there may be three generations in one year it is most important to control the trouble at the start, when it is often seen on baby plants, even on the cotyledons. *Control Measures* Spray with nicotine and soft soap (or substitute spreader) directly the trouble is seen. Give another spraying a week later. Spray on a warm day if possible.
Formula: $\frac{1}{4}$ oz liquid nicotine, $\frac{1}{4}$ lb soft soap, $2\frac{1}{2}$ gal. water.
This pest also attacks spinach.

Other pests that may attack beetroot are Eelworm (See **Pea**), Flea Beetles (see **Cabbage**), Black Aphis (See **Bean, Broad**).

Cabbage

APHIS, MEALY CABBAGE (*Brevicoryne brassicae*)
This is a very serious pest which attacks all members of the cabbage family. So serious is it in the counties of Bedfordshire, Cambridgeshire and Huntingdon that the Ministry of Agriculture have issued compulsory orders with regard to its control.

The aphis is of a mealy, mauve colour. It distorts the leaves of plants and reduces the rate of growth. It is usually found on the under-surface of leaves and in the case of Brussels sprouts, gets right into the hearts. The aphids, too, may be found in blisters on the underside of foliage. *Control Measures* As the aphids often live on Brussels sprouts etc., all through the winter, and may lay eggs on winter greens, it is suggested that all sprout plants and seed plants which provide the main source of infestation, should be sprayed or dusted with nicotine early in May. The summer planted crop should be dealt with as the infestation arises.

The spraying with nicotine and soft soap should always be

done at least a fortnight before cutting, so as to allow the
nicotine to be vaporised or washed off before the sprouts or
cabbage are eaten. Derris sprays may be used by those who
fear to use nicotine.

BEETLES, FLEA

Flea beetles are small and generally black or dark grey in
colour. They damage young plants when they are first coming
through the ground and they may nibble them off just below
the ground. They attack the leaves of larger plants, causing
them to look punctured and distorted.

They can be easily recognised because they hop away
quickly and hide themselves when disturbed. They will even
do this when the shadow of the gardener falls upon them.
Large numbers of them attacking plants may cause them to
look quite black.

Flea beetles spend the winter in dry, vegetable rubbish such
as is found in hedge bottoms and under stacks of straw. They
commence attacking plants early in May and may continue to
do so well on into August. *Control Measures* The seeds of all
members of the cabbage family, including turnip, swede and
radish, should be wetted with paraffin at the rate of $\frac{1}{8}$ pt per $\frac{1}{2}$
lb. seed used. The seed should then be dried overnight and
sown the next day.

Derris dust applied liberally is perfectly effective. It should
be applied on to the rows as soon as the seedlings have
appeared through the soil. A second dusting is advisable a
week later according to weather conditions.

CABBAGE ROOT FLY (*Delia brassicae*)

This pest is very widely distributed and is perhaps the most
important of all those that attack cabbage, cauliflower,
Brussels sprout and broccoli. There are at least two generations a year and under exceptional conditions a third may
occur.

The maggots attack the cabbages in the roots and stem. The
eggs are laid at soil level and the larvae on hatching out then
burrows up and down in the pith. Plants that have been
attacked remain small as the root is unable to develop. *Control
Measures* Buy tarred roofing felt. Cut it into four-inch squares.
Make a slit in each one on one side of the square right to the
centre. Slip the felt around the stem of each cabbage up to the
split at planting time. This prevents the cabbage root fly from

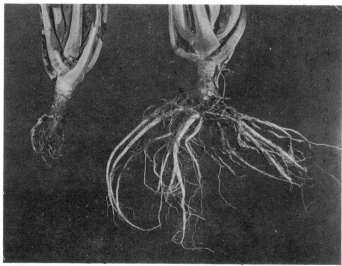

Cabbage root fly on cauliflowers; the left hand plant badly attacked

laying her eggs on the stem just below the soil surface. These squares of roofing felt may be taken up in August and can be used again the following season. With care they should last for years. (See figure 22). Compost growing does reduce attacks of root fly.

CABBAGE WHITEFLY (*Aleurodes brassicae*)
These whiteflies are similar to those found in the greenhouse. These white waxy flies are usually found on the under surface of leaves. They suck the sap and make the plants unpalatable because of the 'frass' they exude. *Control Measures* See Aphis, Mealy Cabbage above.

CABBAGE CATERPILLAR (Cabbage Moth, *Mamestra brassicae* White Butterfly, *Pieris brassicae* and *P. rapae*)
The caterpillars that attack all members of the brassica family including cabbage, Brussels sprout, cauliflower, nasturtium, stock and such weeds as charlock, arise from white butterflies and cabbage moths. The damage they do is similar. The foliage is eaten and the plants are ruined by objectionable excreta.

In the case of the butterfly caterpillars, there are two broods, the second occurring in August and September. The caterpillars tend to feed together and, as a result, they often strip the leaves, leaving only the main ribs and main veins. They usually concentrate on outer leaves.

The caterpillars of the cabbage moth, however, tend to burrow down into the hearts of cabbages and do greater damage in a shorter time than their 'cousins'. They do the greatest amount of damage from June to September. *Control Measures* In both cases the caterpillars can easily be controlled by spraying with liquid derris or dusting with fresh derris powder. It is important to make applications directly the pest is seen for the younger caterpillars are more readily killed than their maturer brothers.

Another effective control is by the application of a Derris dust. The cabbage moth caterpillars should, of course, be dusted before it has eaten its way into the heart of the cabbage where it is inaccessible.

Where a mature caterpillar is found lying comatose surrounded by a mass of little yellow cocoons – this should be left. The cocoons will be the means of ensuring more parasitic 'wasps' which are the natural enemies of this pest.

Carrot

CARROT FLY (*Psila rosae*)
Undoubtedly this is the most serious pest of carrots. It will also attack parsley and celery. The fly is small, dark and of a deep shiny bottle-green colour. The females lay their eggs near the surface of the ground and the larvae burrow under the soil and tunnel into the roots. Large numbers of yellowish maggots may be found in each carrot. The foliage then goes reddish or rusty, the tops may wilt, and the growth of the whole plant is arrested. *Control Measures* Crude or whizzed naphthalene should be applied in between the rows at the rate of 1 oz per yd run, just before thinning and again ten days later. A further dressing should be made a week after this.

Carrots should always be thinned early and the soil compressed along the rows afterwards so as to prevent egg-laying and subsequent movement of larvae. All thinned carrots removed from the rows should be put on the compost heap for rotting down.

Routine spraying of the foliage with a concentration of a 2 per cent solution of garlic oil has given good results. Begin when the carrots have about four leaves and carry on at regular intervals of about twenty-one days till mid September for maincrop carrots.

Sowing the rows of carrots in between rows of onions usually does the trick as the 'scent' of the carrots is masked by the smell of the onions. Thus the carrot fly is not attracted to come and lay her eggs.

CARROT APHIDS (*Cavariella spp*)

The green aphis – commonly known as greenfly – may attack the leaves of carrots in the summer and cause the leaves to turn yellow. *Control Measures* Spray the foliage with nicotine and soft soap.

Formula $\frac{1}{4}$ oz nicotine, $\frac{1}{4}$ lb. soft soap, $2\frac{1}{2}$ gal. water. Give a good soaking on a warm day if possible.

Dusting with a good nicotine dust is also successful, if done on a warm day.

Cabbage stem weevil maggots in stem of old cabbage leaf.
(Plant Protection)

Cauliflower

CABBAGE STEM FLEA BEETLE (*Psylliodes chrysocephala*)
This pest is more serious in the south of England than in the north. The grubs of this beetle tunnel into the stems of young plants and then into the leaf stalks. The plants flag and amateurs often pull them up without noticing where the damage is done.

As the pest will attack young plants in the nursery beds it is possible to put out plants into their permanent position after the grubs have started burrowing. Whole crops have been ruined because of this. *Control Measures* The soil in the nursery beds should be given a good dusting with one of the best proprietary naphthalene dusts before seed sowing. Directly the plants are through, a further dusting should be given and yet another ten days after this. This work should be done early in the morning in each case. Many gardeners now dust with naphthalene as an 'insurance' every year.

Celery

CELERY FLY (*Acidia heraclei*)
The first flies appear in April or May and three broods arise during the season. The first usually in May or early June, the second in late July and the third in September.

The celery fly lays its eggs on the under-surfaces of the leaves. These hatch out into maggots which burrow between the upper and lower surfaces of the foliage, causing blisters. Inside the blisters the maggots feed and grow. It is usually by these blisters, either large or small, that the trouble is first recognised.

The attack generally takes place in the seedling stage, though it is usually not recognised until the second brood appears. *Control Measures* It is most important to protect the young plants in the frames or greenhouse by keeping them sprayed with nicotine and soft soap.

Formula: $\frac{1}{4}$ oz nicotine, $\frac{1}{4}$ lb. soft soap (or spreader), to $2\frac{1}{2}$ gal. water. Hand picking and pinching to destroy the maggots may, of course, be done on a small scale.

Attacked plants may be given a stimulant such as dried blood in order to encourage quick growth. The slightest sprinkling will do.

Once the plants are in their trenches, spraying with nicotine is necessary early in June, as a rule, to control the second generation. If this is properly done, there can be no third generation in September.

Other pests that attack celery are Aphids and Carrot Fly. (See **Carrot**).

Cucumber

RED SPIDER (*Tetranychus telarius*)
A tiny reddish-yellow mite – lives on the under-surfaces of the leaves, sucking the sap and spinning minute white webs. These can usually only be distinguished under a magnifying glass. As a result, the leaves soon turn yellow, and finally a reddish-brown colour. *Control Measures* During the summer see that the under-surfaces of the leaves are syringed regularly with water. Apply the spray with as much force as possible.

In bad attacks it is possible to spray with a summer petroleum oil, used according to the manufacturer's instructions. (See also the section on cucumbers in chapter 14).

ROOT KNOT EELWORM (*Heterodera radicicola*)
A minute eelworm attacks the roots of cucumbers growing in frames and glasshouses. The plants wilt and, if the roots are examined, knot-like galls will be found. Growth is stunted, both above and below ground.

For general details about eelworms, see chapter 3. *Control Measures* No effective method of control is known other than soil sterilisation by heat or steam. For details, see chapter 12.

Lettuce

APHIDS (*Myzus lactucae* etc.)
Several species of aphids live on the leaves of lettuce, both under glass and out of doors. When infested, the leaves become curled and blistered and the plants are stunted. The honeydew exuded from the cornicles of the insects forms a sticky layer over the leaves, to which the cast aphid skins adhere. Another species lives on the roots and can thus cause loss of plants in dry summers.

Besides damaging the plants, these aphids spread viruses that cause stunting and leaf distortion. The three species of aphid most commonly harmful to lettuce are (1) lettuce aphid (2) peach-potato aphid and (3) lettuce root aphid.

Tomato root-knot eelworm showing 'grape' stage of roots
(Plant Protection)

THE LETTUCE APHID

The lettuce aphid is the chief pest of lettuces both in glasshouses and out of doors. The winged and wingless forms are green with black markings. The eggs are laid in the late autumn on the twigs of gooseberries and currants. The eggs hatch in early spring and start colonies on the young leaves, causing leaf-curl. In May winged aphids appear which leave the currants and gooseberries and fly to lettuces. Many aphids

are produced until September and October. The winged
aphids then return to the winter host plants where eggs are
laid.

However, in *most* years in the south the breeding of summer
aphids continues on outdoor lettuce throughout the winter.

THE PEACH-POTATO APHID

The peach-potato aphid is abundant and widespread. It
usually colonises the outside leaves and does little damage. It
is, however, the vector of the lettuce mosaic virus. It over-
winters in the egg stage on peach or nectarine trees and often
as wingless females on savoys. Wingless females also over-
winter on lettuce in glasshouses, frames, and under cloches.

THE LETTUCE ROOT APHID

The lettuce root aphid is harmful to outdoor lettuce in the
summer. It lays its eggs on the Lombardy and Black poplar
where, in spring time the newly hatched insects live inside
galls on the leaf stalks. During June winged aphids develop in
the galls. These dry and split. The first few generations of
wingless aphids appear on the roots of lettuces and sow-
thistles.

In late summer and autumn the generation of winged
aphids migrates from lettuce to the poplars. A few root aphids
may live in the winter in the soil and so colonise lettuces
planted in the same ground in the spring.

THE POTATO APHID etc.

Three other species of aphid feed on lettuces. These are the
potato aphid, the glasshouse-potato aphid and the shallot
aphid, but only the potato aphid causes much damage to
outdoor lettuces. All three can be pests of lettuces under glass
right through the year.

PREDATORS

Aphids infesting outdoor lettuce are attacked by grubs of
hover flies, by ladybirds and their niggers and by minute
wasp-like parasites. These insect parasites and predators are,
however, much less active in the winter. At all times of the year
lettuce aphids are liable to destruction by parasitic fungi.
Because Lombardy poplar is a winter host of the lettuce root
aphid, do not plant these trees in a vegetable garden.

When applying nicotine sprays or nicotine dust, care should
be taken to aim at the hearts of the plants and the undersides
of the leaves.

OUTDOOR CROPS

WINTER LETTUCE

All useless old lettuces near a proposed winter lettuce bed should be pulled up and composted. Seedbeds should be treated with nicotine to ensure that aphid-free seedlings are transplanted. If thoroughly treated, the crop will remain clean until cutting time, because reinfestation by winged aphids does not take place on a large scale before May.

SUMMER LETTUCE

The control of aphids in the outdoor summer lettuces is more costly because migrant aphids may reinfest the crop almost any time from May to September. To ensure that clean lettuce is marketed the crop must be examined periodically for aphids. If aphid colonies are found the crop should be sprayed with nicotine and soft soap (usual formula) on a sunny day. Examination of the plants should continue to within a week of cutting.

If aphids are carrying the mosaic virus, the infection usually occurs before the aphids can be killed. Aphid control *after* migration is not, therefore, a means of controlling lettuce or cucumber mosaic. Hence all crops must be kept clean throughout their life, weed control must be thorough also. *Control Measures* Spray with nicotine on a warm day.

Formula: $\frac{1}{4}$ oz nicotine, $\frac{1}{4}$ lb. soft soap to $2\frac{1}{2}$ gal. water. Spray the soil all round also, so that nicotine fumes will arise and kill the insects. Nicotine dusts may be used.

In the case of lettuce root aphids, before planting out lettuces in the summer or sowing lettuce seed, crude or whizzed naphthalene may be forked into the ground at 3 oz to the sq. yd. This will usually keep the aphids away. A further dressing may be hoed into the ground when the plants are an inch high or so, if necessary. Other pests that attack lettuces are slugs (see chapter 3).

Mushroom

MUSHROOM FLIES

Many species of flies will damage mushrooms, the *Sciara* and the *Phorid* being the most important. They are similar in size – the larvae tunnel into the mushrooms as they appear, ruining both the stems and the caps as well. Their ravages make the mushrooms quite unsaleable, and bad attacks can easily destroy the whole crop. *Control Measures* Relatively low temperatures in the house may prevent egg-laying and retard the development of the flies. The temperature should be kept just below 60°F.

Strict cleanliness should be observed.

Apply pyrethrum dust at 1 oz per sq. yd to the beds before spawning, and again when the casing soil is in place over the spawned bed or use a Pysect aerosol.

MUSHROOM MITES

There are a large number of mites that may be found in a mushroom house. The slow moving species are usually the most harmful, while the active ones are normally harmless.

They attack as soon as the mushrooms start to appear, holes being found in the stalks and the caps. These holes, when examined under a magnifying glass, will be found to contain numerous eggs and mites. These mites may injure the spawn as well, so cropping may thus cease. *Control Measures* Fresh manure is probably less likely to contain injurious mites than that which has been stored for a long period.

Onion

ONION FLY (*Delia* (*Hylemyia*) *antiqua*)

The onion fly is similar to the ordinary house-fly. It is a little over $\frac{1}{4}$ in. long, dark grey in colour, and has tiny red eyes and black legs.

The female lays several eggs on the soil or on the neck of the onion early in May. She is attracted to the onion rows by the strong smell. The maggots usually hatch out in five to seven days. They are dirty white in colour, have no legs, and when full grown are about $\frac{1}{3}$ in. long.

The first indication of infestation is usually the flagging of the plants and the yellowing of the leaves. *Control Measures* Crude naphthalene should be applied along the rows at the rate of 2 oz to the yd run. The first application should be made just before thinning, and a further application ten days later.

Always sow onions in between rows of carrots and then the maggots are confused by the carroty smell and so keep away.

Parsnip

Parsnips are attacked by the celery fly, but it is seldom that the trouble is very serious. As, however, this may prove a breeding-ground for attacks on celery, it is worthwhile controlling it. (See **Celery**).

Other pests that attack parsnips are Carrot Fly (see **Carrot**) and aphides (see chapter 3).

Spraying the parsnips with a garlic spray as advised for Carrot will keep the females from laying their eggs on the parsnip leaves.

Pea

PEA AND BEAN BEETLES (*Bruchus spp*)

The beetles lay eggs on the pods and the maggots which hatch out in a few days burrow into the peas themselves and feed on them. When sowing pea seeds, little beetles may be found among them. *Control Measures* Where infected seed is suspected it should be placed in a little muslin bag which can be hung from the end of a stick into boiling water for five seconds.

Be sure that the water is boiling and do not leave the peas in the water longer than the specified time.

PEA MOTH (*Cydia (Graphoipha) nigricana*)

The female of the pea moth lays its eggs on the young pods, and the larvae soon burrow into the pods and destroy the peas. Three or four larvae may be found in a pod, feeding on the seeds. When these are fully grown, they drop to the ground and pupate in the soil. The moths emerge from these cocoons early next summer. *Control Measures* The young pods should be sprayed with nicotine as the flowers are setting. Any moths about are then killed and the larvae or eggs on the outside of the pods are killed also.

Continuous cultivation is also important for by this means the larvae are exposed when they drop to the ground and will be eaten by birds.

A rotation of crops should be carried out as this hinders infection.

PEA AND BEAN WEEVILS (*Sitona lineatus* and other spp)

It is thought that the larvae live in the soil and feed on the little white nodules which are found on the roots of all members of the pea and bean family. The weevils themselves eat semi-circular notches out of the sides and edges of the leaves. A great deal of damage can thus be done to young plants.

The weevils are dark grey in colour and are almost indistinguishable in the soil. For this reason the damage done is often attributed to birds. *Control Measures* By regular hoeing ensure a fine tilth along the rows and thus remove the clods of soil which are the natural hiding place of the weevil. Regular cultivation disturbs them also and they dislike this.

Dust liberally with a derris dust when the damage is first seen.

PEA APHIS (*Macrosiphum pisi*)

This is a small aphis (greenfly), green in colour, similar to the fly which attacks broad beans. It usually attacks peas when they are young and three quarters grown. Seldom attacks fully grown plants. *Control Measures* Spray with nicotine and soft soap.

Formula: $\frac{1}{4}$ oz nicotine, $\frac{1}{4}$ lb. soft soap to $2\frac{1}{2}$ gal. water, directly the first aphides are seen.

Or, spray with liquid Derris giving the rows a thorough soaking.

EELWORMS (*Heterodera schachtii* and *Anguillulina dipsaci*)
See Eelworms, chapter 3.

Heterodera attacks the roots, forming little cysts on them similar to, but smaller than, the bacterial nodules found on the roots of all pea and bean plants. *Control Measures* No control is at present known. Peas should not be grown on the same ground for four years.

PEA AND BEAN THRIPS (*Kakothrips pisirorus*)
See Thrips, chapter 3.

Pea and bean thrips first attack the seedlings, sucking the sap from the growing points. The plants are thus distorted and the growth is limited. Later, they attack the leaves, stems and pods and, in a dry season, they multiply rapidly.

The pods become silvery looking, and later turn brown. The trouble usually begins near the base of the plants and, in bad cases, the pods are small and distorted. *Control Measures* Hoe regularly along the rows. Before planting, apply garden lime at 5 oz to the sq. yd, after liming cover the soil with powdery compost or sedge peat and this will make hoeing unnecessary.

Three weeks before picking, when the majority of the flowers have set, spray the rows with nicotine and soft soap.

Formula: $\frac{1}{4}$ oz nicotine, $\frac{1}{4}$ lb. soft soap to $2\frac{1}{2}$ gal. water.
Other pests that attack peas are Slugs. (See chapter 3).

Potato

THE COLORADO BEETLE

At the present time Colorado Beetles have only been found in the south of this country. They are, however, a very dangerous potato pest.

The beetle spends the winter buried in the soil to a depth of ten inches. Late in the spring or early in the summer it works its way to the surface and flies to the nearest potato plant. It feeds on the potato leaves, the females laying clusters of eggs at the same time. These hatch out into grubs which feed on the leaves also. In three weeks these are fully grown, and they burrow in the soil to pupate. Ten days later they may emerge again as adult beetles. They will then burrow up to the surface and produce a further generation.

In bad attacks all the tops of the potatoes will be eaten and no tubers worth digging will be formed. The beetles are similar in size and shape to ladybirds, but are bright yellow and have black stripes running from one end to the other of their bodies. The larvae are reddish orange in colour and have three pairs of legs. *Control Measures* Any suspected Colorado beetle or grubs should be placed in a tin box with no holes punched in it, together with a piece of potato leaf. This should be sent immediately to the Ministry of Agriculture, 28 Milton Road, Harpenden, Herts, with a letter stating the exact place where the insects were found and the name and address of the finder. No other steps should be taken until the Ministry give instructions.

See also Slugs, Wireworms in chapter 3.

Radish

CABBAGE WHITEFLY, FLEA BEETLES AND ROOT FLY
See **Cabbage.**

Spinach

MANGOLD FLY
See **Beetroot.**

Turnip

TURNIP GALL WEEVIL (*Ceuthorrhynchus pleurostigma*)
This gall weevil attacks all members of the cabbage family, such as cabbage, savoy, Brussels sprout, kale, kohl-rabi, as well as turnip. When attacked, the plants produce large rounded galls which grow out from the root, usually near ground-level. These galls or 'hard blisters' when cut open, will be found to be hollow and to contain a white grub. This may be white or yellowish and is legless with a brown head. When found it is usually curled up.

The beetle itself is only $\frac{1}{8}$ in. long, is black above and greyish underneath.

Many people confuse turnip gall weevil with Club Root, but it is the presence of the little curled-up maggot in the galls that helps to show the difference. The 'galls' produced by the Club Root disease are usually larger and when cut open are very evil smelling. (See **Club Root**.)

CONTROL MEASURES
Use affected turnips as soon as possible, as in this way the maggots can be destroyed before they leave the galls and pupate in the ground.

All cabbage stems etc., affected by these galls should be composted properly, so as to kill the maggots. This means bashing the stems with the back of an axe on a chopping block.

Dust along the rows in August with powdered naphthalene at 1 oz to the yd run.

6   The diseases of vegetables

Asparagus

ASPARAGUS RUST (*Puccinia asparagi*)
This rust usually appears after midsummer. First of all, rusty spots are seen on the stems which look blistered. The little leaves which should be glossy green turn yellowish brown. As the autumn approaches, the spots look darker. *Control Measures* The foliage should be cut in the autumn, before the little leaves, known as needles, fall. The material should then be burnt immediately. The cut should be made just below soil level, so that no portion of the stem is left above ground to serve as a source of infection the following year.

Young plants should always be raised as far away as possible from the established beds, with the object of preventing infection taking place. Two resistant varieties are *Martha Washington* and *Mary Washington*.
Special Note: gardeners sometimes call a streaky looking discoloration of the white stem at cutting time, rust. The rust is just a blemish and should not be confused with the disease.

VIOLET ROOT ROT (*Rhizoctonia crocorum*)
This root rot attacks the underground portions of asparagus plants and is commonly called by gardeners 'Copper-web' or 'Coppery-web'. The crowns become covered with a brownish purple spawn and, as a result of an attack, the plants are soon exhausted and die. Unfortunately, the disease is often not noticed until the plants are seen to be dying off in circular areas several feet in diameter. *Control Measures* Contaminated soil may be treated by forking in bleaching powder at the rate of 2 oz to the sq. yd either late in the spring or early in the summer. All affected roots should be burnt; in bad cases the whole of the asparagus bed should be scrapped and burnt.
Special Note: This disease also attacks beetroot, carrot, mangold, potato and, on farms, clover and lucerne. None of these crops should be grown on land which has grown infected asparagus.

Beetroot

BLACK LEG (*Phoma betae, Pythium de baryanum, Pythium aphamidermatum* and *Corticium solani*)
All these diseases may cause young seedlings to damp off and the stems to become blackened as a result. Large numbers of seedings may die at a time. In bad attacks the roots, instead of being thick and round, are thread-like.

The trouble is usually contracted from the seed. *Control Measures* The seed should be treated with formalin. See **Celery**.

HEART ROT (A functional disorder)
In July the leaves in the crown of the beetroot turn black and die and, in bad cases, the outer leaves will be killed also. Subsequently the root will rot away.

It is a particularly bad disease in dry summers and on soils that have been heavily limed. *Control Measures* It is better to grow beetroot on land that contains sufficient organic and moisture-holding matter. Heavy dressings of lime should not be given.

Borax should be applied to the ground at the rate of $\frac{1}{8}$ oz to the sq. yd before sowing the seed on land which is suspected of producing Heart Rot. It is said that this desease is due to a deficiency of boron.

LEAF SPOT (*Cercospora beticola*)
This trouble is usually present wherever beetroot is grown. On farms it is found also on sugar beet and mangold wurzel.

Spots will be found on the leaves, first of all brown, with reddish-purple borders and then, when these reach $\frac{1}{8}$ in. in size, they become grey in the centre. Later, the dead tissue will drop out leaving a ragged hole. *Control Measures* After an infected crop has been harvested, all the leaves should be burnt or dug in at least a spade's depth.

In severe cases spray the rows with a Bordeaux mixture using 1 lb. powdered copper sulphate, $1\frac{1}{2}$ lb. garden lime to $12\frac{1}{2}$ gal. water. It is necessary to spray again a fortnight afterwards and again a fortnight after that.

A proprietary Bordeaux spray may be used for the purpose.

As the disease is seed-borne, all seed thought to be infected should be soaked in formaldehyde.

Formula: 3 parts formaldehyde to 200 parts of water – for 7

minutes. It should then be rinsed with water and either dried or sown at once. Other diseases which will attack beetroot are Crown Gall, which may cause large ugly swellings. No method of control is known. Violet Root Rot (see **Asparagus**), Common Scab (see **Potato**) and Rust (*Uromyces betae*).

Bean, Broad

CHOCOLATE SPOT
The stems, foliage and pods of the broad beans are covered with dark brown spots, blotches or streaks. The trouble is usually worse in rainy seasons. *Control Measures* Applications of potash before sowing the seed seem to make the plants more resistant to the disease.

Therefore, fork in wood ashes at 8 oz to the sq. yd, plus bone meal at 5 oz to the sq. yd, giving the surface of the soil a dressing of garden lime at 5 oz to the sq. yd afterwards. Other diseases that may attack broad beans are Rust (*Uromyces fabae*). This seldom gives trouble until the plants are fully grown, when it does little harm. It can be controlled if necessary by spraying with colloidal copper. For Leaf Spot (*Cercospora fabae*) see **Beetroot**.

Bean, Dwarf

ANTHRACNOSE (*Colletotrichum lindemuthianum*)
This disease is found all over the country. It is sometimes called Canker, other times Rust, and even Blight. Small dark specks will be found on the pods, leaves and stems. They are usually surrounded by reddish lines. The spots get larger and become more regularly shaped, looking like sunken brown patches. These, in their turn, are covered later with a thin, whitish crust. The disease is at its worst during cold, wet weather.

Badly affected plants are often shrivelled and spotted beans, when sown, may either not germinate at all or produce a stem which drops its cotyledons. The cankers on the stems sometimes are so numerous and so deep as to cause the plant to fall over. It is, however, the spot on the pod which is most obvious and which does the greatest amount of harm. *Control Measures* The plants should be sprayed as a precaution, before the first pods set, with Bordeaux mixture at half the normal strength, i.e. $\frac{1}{2}$ lb. powdered copper sulphate, $\frac{3}{4}$ lb. garden lime, to $12\frac{1}{2}$ gal. water. Mix in a plastic container.

Further sprayings should be given, if necessary, with liver of sulphur, dissolving $\frac{1}{2}$ oz in a 2-gal. can of water. It is never, however, advisable to spray after the pods are half grown.

HALO BLIGHT (*Bacterium medicaginis*)
When attacked by Halo Blight the whole of the plant or part of it suddenly wilts. Small, angular spots surrounded by a light 'halo' appear, not only on the leaves, but also on the stems and pods. Sometimes a milky fluid exudes from the spots. *Control Measures* It is most important to sow clean seed. Affected seeds are wrinkled, blistered and/or have yellow spots on them. All affected plants should be removed and burnt directly they are seen. Infected ground should be 'rested' for 4 years – i.e. don't grow dwarf beans on such land for 4 years.

The variety *Black Wonder* has been shown to be fairly resistant.

MOSAIC
A virus disease which produces irregular light yellow areas, and dark green patches on the leaves. This mottling or mosaic effect causes the leaves to become puckered, especially along the mid-rib. The leaf usually curls downwards.

As far as is known, the virus lives through the winter in the seed. It may be transmitted from plant to plant during picking or by the ravages of insects. *Control Measures* No control methods are known at present.

Bean, Runner
See **Dwarf, Bean.**
Special Note: Halo Blight does not seem troublesome.

Cabbage

CLUB ROOT (*Plasmodiophora brassicae*)
See chapter 4.

CANKER (*Phoma lingam*)
Sometimes called Black Leg. It attacks all types of cabbage, as well as turnip, kohl-rabi, mustard, radish, cress and even sweet alyssum.

The plants may either become infected in the seed-bed or later in the summer. A depressed light brown canker will be found near the base of the stem. This enlarges until the stem is girdled. The tissue will then turn black, while light brown circular spots may appear on the leaves.

In bad cases the plants will wilt or, if the attack is late in the season, the weight of the plant may cause it to lean over. *Control Measures* No member of the cabbage family should be grown on affected land for three years.

Dip the seed in water at a temperature of 122°F. for 30 minutes. The seed should then be removed, dipped in cold water to cool and be spread out to dry afterwards. Unfortunately, this treatment usually reduces germination.

RING SPOT (*Mycosphaerella brassicicola*)

A disease mainly of the southern and south-western counties of England, though it occurs also in Wales. Prefers to attack broccoli.

Circular brown spots surrounded by a green border appear on the leaves, varying in size from $\frac{1}{10}-\frac{1}{2}$ in. Mainly abundant on the lower leaves. *Control Measures* Remove the older leaves and the outer leaves immediately any sign of the trouble is seen. Burn all refuse removed from affected plants. Do not grow members of the cabbage family on the same piece of ground for three or four years.

DOWNY MILDEW (*Peronospora parasitica*)

This damages seedlings rather than well-grown plants. Particularly bad on cauliflowers, especially so in the case of plants raised under glass.

The leaves turn yellowish green in colour and when examined closely, white downy patches will be seen on the under-surfaces. *Control Measures* Spray with liver of sulphur.

Formula: 1 oz potassium sulphide to 2 gal. water. Avoid overcrowding at all costs.

Other diseases that may attack cabbages are Leaf Spot, Soft Rot, White Blister and Grey Mould. None of these is very serious and no practicable control measures are yet known in connection with any of them.

Carrot

SCLEROTINIA ROT (*Sclerotinia sclerotiorum*)

A rot which occurs in storage bins, in clamps, 'burys', 'hales', 'hogs' and pits. The roots shrink and rot because they are attacked by this fungus disease near the crown as the result of direct infection from the soil. *Control Measures* Never attempt to store any roots which have been 'wounded' in any way during harvesting. Roots which show any indication of the disease before storage should be burnt together with any other infected material.

Good ventilation discourages the development of this fungus.

Other diseases that may attack carrots are Violet Root Rot (see **Asparagus**); Soft Rot (see **Celery**). When in store the roots may be given a light dusting with Bordeaux powder. This of course must be washed off before using the roots.

Cauliflower
(See **Cabbage**)

Celery

LEAF SPOT (*Septoria apii*)
Undoubtedly the most serious disease of celery. It appears all over the country and has caused complete crop failure.

On the foliage discoloured areas will be found on which minute black fluted bodies will be seen. The spots will increase in size until the whole leaf is affected. It will then wither away and rot. Sometimes this disease appears as brown, dry patches, plus a few black specks.

Though the disease usually attacks the plants in the early stages, it is generally not obvious until July. The disease is carried on from year to year by infected seed. *Control Measures* Seed should be purchased from seedsmen who guarantee that the seed coats are free from the disease, or all celery seeds purchased should be soaked in a weak solution of formaldehyde for 24 hours.

Formula: 1 part of formalin to 300 parts of water. The seed should be dried slowly afterwards.

In the garden, the plants should be sprayed with Bordeaux mixture, making certain to give them a thorough covering, both the lower and upper surfaces of the leaves. In most years three applications are necessary to get complete control. In wet years more applications than this may be advisable.

Formula: $1\frac{1}{2}$ lb. garden lime, 1 lb. copper sulphate to $12\frac{1}{2}$ gal. water. Alternatively, a copper white oil emulsion spray may be used.

ROOT ROT (*Phoma apiicola*)
Attacked plants develop black or dark brown areas, both on the roots and on the stems just below soil level. In very bad cases the tops of the plants will break off. The trouble may occur both on the seedlings and on the adult plants. This disease is common all over the country. It is carried on from year to year on the seed coats. *Control Measures* It is possible now to obtain seed which is guaranteed to be free from this disease. Seedsmen should be asked about this. Where infected seed is purchased this should be treated with formalin as advised for leaf spot.

SOFT ROT (*Bacterium carotovorum*)
This rot usually attacks the hearts of celery plants, rendering them useless. The trouble generally occurs from December onwards, and will continue even though the adult celery plants are lifted to be stored under cover. The disease enters the plants through wounds made by insects, slugs and snails. *Control Measures* All insects, slugs and snails should be kept down. Affected plants should be burnt and the ground concerned should not be used for growing celery for three years.

Apply borax crystals along the rows before planting at $\frac{1}{8}$ oz to the yd run and raking lightly in has proved useful.

Cucumber

ANTHRACNOSE (*Colletotrichum lagenarium*)
This disease is often called Leaf Spot because the foliage when attacked is covered by reddish or pale green spots. These enlarge and unite, and the leaves then wither and die. The stems and fruits may be attacked too.

It is the most widespread serious leaf spot disease of cucumbers in the country. *Control Measures* The fungus will live on new and rotten wood; on paper, straw and even on strawy manure. The spores will be spread when watering and syringing and distributed on the clothes of workers.

Excessive humidity in the glasshouse or frame should be avoided and so should wide variations of temperatures.

Spray affected plants directly the first signs of the disease are noticed with liver of sulphur.

Formula: 1 oz potassium sulphide to 2 gal. water, stirring in a cupful of flour paste. Regular spraying every week may be necessary.

BLOTCH (*Cercospora melonis*)

A disease which was very prevalent in the country but which has almost disappeared now since the introduction of the variety Butcher's Disease Resister.

Pale green, water-soaked spots appear on the leaves. These turn brown and soon the leaves wither completely. Can soon ruin a whole plant. *Control Measures* An immune variety like Butcher's Disease Resisting should be obtained from the seedsman. The soil should always be sterilised (see chapter 12). Cucumbers should not be grown with too much humidity or in too high temperatures.

CANKER (*Bacterium carotovorum*)

A brown soft rot or canker occurs just below or just above soil level. Sometimes the disease attacks young plants but generally it doesn't show itself till the plants are fruiting.

The trouble is usually caused by wet conditions of the soil where the base of the plants join the soil. *Control Measures* Keep the base of the plant as dry as possible. Never allow any water to be poured directly on the stems.

Dust the stems which are invariably the parts affected, with a mixture consisting of 10 parts garden lime, 3 parts finely divided copper sulphate and 3 parts flowers of sulphur.

FUSARIUM WILT (*Fusarium sp*)

This causes wilting, yellowing and desiccation of the leaves. Usually starts from the base and works upwards, causing the death of the plant. Develops most rapidly with high soil temperatures. *Control Measures* Sterilise all soil before using (see chapter 12).

Remove infected plants, together with the soil around their roots. The holes thus made may be filled in with a mixture of 8 parts soil and 1 part lime. This should then be watered with a Cheshunt Compound solution and replanted with a young cucumber plant.

GREY MOULD (*Botrytis cinerea*)

Grey velvety fungus growth will appear over the leaves and even over the stems. May also damage the young fruits. *Control Measures* As the trouble is only severe under very humid conditions it is necessary to pay adequate attention to ventilation and to general plant hygiene.

GUMMOSIS (*Cladosporium cucumerinum*)
Attacks the fruits only, causing small sunken spots to appear. These soon enlarge and exude a gummy liquid. A dark olive-green, velvety growth then covers the affected parts. Cracks may appear and the white flesh below may be exposed. In very bad cases the fungus will attack the leaves, causing small, light brown spots to appear. *Control Measures* Remove all deseased fruits and leaves immediately they are seen, and burn them.

As the disease is most destructive under humid conditions, give more air by attending to ventilation.

Spray with liver of sulphur.

Formula: 1 oz of potassium sulphide to 5 gal. water, stirring in a cupful of flour paste.

MOSAIC
There are various viruses which attack cucumbers known as Mosaic. The commonest, often called Green Mottle, causes the leaves to be mottled, wrinkled and puckered. The plants are dwarfed also. Another, known as yellow mosaic, causes yellow mottling of the leaves, plus silver-coloured or yellow streaks and spots on the fruit. The plants are also stunted. *Control Measures* Purchase virus-free seed. Insect pests should be kept down at all costs because these transmit the virus. The virus may be carried on the fingers or knives of the gardeners.

VERTICILLIUM WILT (*Verticillium albo-atrum*)
Will attack tomatoes as well as cucumbers. The damage is chiefly done early in the spring and late in the autumn when the temperature is low.

The symptoms produced are similar to those of Fusarium Wilt (see above) and, on cutting open diseased stems, the wood will be found to be of yellowish-brown colour. *Control Measures* Raise the temperature of the house to 77°F.

Avoid any heavy watering.

Leek

RUST (*Puccinia porri*)
This disease is common in most parts of England and Wales but is particularly bad in the north.

Yellowish spots, scattered or arranged more or less in rows, will be found on the foliage. These gradually turn yellowish red. *Control Measures* Do not plant leeks on the same ground for four or five years. Remove affected leaves and burn them or, in bad cases, whole plants.

Spraying with colloidal copper is a possible cure.

WHITE TIP (*Phytophthora porri*)
This disease is bad in market-gardens around Edinburgh and in the Evesham valley. It is known, however, to attack plants all over the country.

The ends of the leaves first die back and then turn white. Sometimes the parts attacked are limp and, on other occasions, they remain crisp and stiff. Sometimes the margins of the leaves are damaged and then they become twisted. Water-soaked areas may develop towards the middle or base of the plant. Diseased plants are always badly checked in growth. *Control Measures* Dust the plants with copper-lime at the rate of 2 oz to the sq. yd. Continue dusting at intervals of four weeks from October till early spring.

Cut off infected tips and burn.

Lettuce

DOWNY MILDEW (*Bremia lactucae*)
Affects outdoor plants in damp climates. Often attacks lettuces under glass. The leaves become yellowish and sometimes brown. In bad cases the whole of the plant will be yellow and dwarfed. The mildewy appearance of the leaves will be noted. *Control Measures* Humidity in glasshouses should be avoided. Grow resistant varieties under glass like *Dandie* and *Premier*. Consult the seedsman.

GREY MOULD (*Botrytis cinerea*)
A very common disease of seedlings in the frame. Also causes the rotting of plants in the field, especially in wet seasons.

The plants become covered with a grey mould and as a result they wilt. *Control Measures* It is of the greatest importance to see that the plants are put in 'level' – neither too deep nor too shallow, either in the seed box or out of doors. The plants should, as it were, just sit on the soil. Outside the plants should never be put in with a dibble hole left at the side. All the leaves showing any brown spot should be cut off with a sharp knife.

Diseased plants and decaying rubbish should be removed and burnt.

RING SPOT (*Marssonina panattoniana*)

This causes more losses than any other lettuce disease. It is very prevalent in cold wet weather.

Infection starts in the outer leaves and soon spreads towards the heart and may easily kill a plant. Brown spots appear on the leaves. These soon turn white, the dead portions then dropping out, leaving holes with white margins. Infection usually occurs on the underside of the midribs where rusty brown blotches appear. *Control Measures* Avoid using any manure containing lettuce refuse unless it has been properly composted. Carry out some system of rotation which prevents lettuces being grown on the same ground year after year. Use an artificial manure rich in potash.

Under glass admit more air and reduce the moisture content in the house. Keep up a buoyant atmosphere.

VIRUS DISEASES

LETTUCE MOSAIC

Infected plants are stunted; they fail to heart and the leaves are mottled in various shades of green. In bad cases the whole plant may be yellowish with crinkled leaves.

The disease is spread by several species of aphid which feed on the leaves by sucking the sap and thus carrying the causal virus from infected plants to healthy ones. The lettuce aphid (*Nasonovia ribisnigri*) is not, however, a vector.

The virus is seed transmitted. About 5 per cent of the seed set by infected plants carries the virus and, if these are sown, they give rise to infected seedlings. The virus can be seed transmitted in most varieties, with the exception of *Cheshunt Early Giant*.

Seed transmission is the greatest factor in the introduction of the disease. The spread of the virus occurs, therefore (a) from seedlings infected through the seed and (b) from neighbouring infected lettuce.

The disease can be controlled by making certain that the crop is free from any external sources of virus *and* that the seed used contains less than 0.1 per cent infection. Seed of some varieties with the extremely low infection rate of less than 0.003 per cent can be got and this should always be sown.

BEET WESTERN YELLOWS

A very serious yellowing disease of lettuce which affects

butterhead, crisp and cos summer lettuce crops all over Britain.

The disease usually appears two weeks before cutting when the *outer* leaves develop an interveinal yellowing. The symptoms usually intensify further and then the whole plant becomes yellowish or even white in colour with a brown margin to the outer leaves.

This virus is not seed transmitted nor is it soil-borne. It is readily transmitted by aphids such as the potato-peach aphid, (*Myzus persicae*). The virus can be found in some common weeds and may over-winter in them. It is extremely important therefore to control groundsel and shepherd's purse.

No immune or resistant lettuce varieties are known so that everything possible should be done to kill the aphids which transmit it. Old lettuces and weeds near new lettuce rows should be destroyed before sowing or planting. Plants should be insecticide-treated to keep them aphid-free throughout their life.

Marrow

MILDEW (*Erysiphe cichoracearum*)
The leaves and younger portions of the plant will be covered with a white powdery growth. The plants then wither and the fruiting period is curtailed. *Control Measures* The plants should be dusted as soon as the disease appears with a good sulphur dust. Another method is to spray the plants with a solution of liver of sulphur using 1 oz to 3 gal. soft water.

All badly affected plants should be uprooted and burnt.

Mint

RUST (*Puccinia menthae*)
This disease occurs wherever mint is grown. The plants attacked can be noticed in the spring and summer because the shoots are distorted and abnormally thick. Before long yellowish orange cushions appear on the stems and leaves. These produce innumerable spores which are distributed to other plants which they infect. Rust spreads like an epidemic in the summer.

In the winter dark brown, or almost black, spores are formed. *Control Measures* Burn off the mint tops in late September or early October. Use dry straw for this purpose and produce a rapid fire so as to burn the stems and the leaves.

Another method and a very successful one, too, is to cut the tops down in October, and remove and burn them. Roots that are lifted for forcing should be washed thoroughly in two changes of water. This removes most of the infected material.

It is also well worthwhile washing roots that are to be replanted out of doors in this way. An even more effective method is to subject the roots to hot water treatment. They should be immersed in a bath of water maintained at a temperature of 112°F. for 10 minutes.

Onion

DOWNY MILDEW (*Peronospora destructor*)
A very serious onion disease which occurs most seasons but, in wet years, is particularly bad. The trouble will attack shallots, but seldom leeks. The crop weight is reduced, the keeping quality of the bulbs impaired and, with young plants, many deaths occur. The leaves turn yellow and soon afterwards collapse. The mildew itself is of a whitish-grey colour and looks like felt. The bulb, though it may be overrun with the 'roots' or mycelium of the fungus, seldom shows any external sign. *Control Measures* Never grow onions on low-lying land or any ground that is poorly drained. Never plant out soft onion sets as they may contain the mycelium of the disease. Sow the spring sown crop as far away from the autumn sown crop as possible.

Spray with a Bordeaux mixture (for formula see chapter 13). This prevents the spread of this disease from plant to plant. Dust, if preferred, with copper lime dust.

SMUT (*Urocystis cepulae*)
A very serious disease of onions which is scheduled under the Destructive Insects and Pests Act and therefore its presence on any plants must be notified at once to the Ministry of Agriculture. Plays havoc, particularly with young plants and seedlings.

It may be distinguished by the dark opaque spots and streaks which are seen on the leaves and scales of the plants. Soon afterwards the skin covering these spots will split and a black powdery mass will exude. Most plants die but those which survive develop more leaves on which more blisters occur. The soil will thus become contaminated and may remain so for many years. *Control Measures* Do not grow onions on the same piece of ground for five years. Pull up the plants and burn them directly the trouble is seen to prevent the spores from infecting the soil.

Water the seed drills with a diluted formalin solution.

Formula: 1 part of formalin to 300 parts of water.

WHITE ROT (*Sclerotium cepivorum*)

A fungus disease which rots the bulbs of onions when they are quite small. The damage is done at the roots and no mould develops on the foliage. The disease may appear at the end of April, but is usually seen during the first hot spell in May or June. The infected plants wilt, and when pulled they come away easily from the soil, thus exposing a mass of white mould at the base of the plant.

It is this white mould that distinguishes the trouble from the onion fly maggot attack. The disease may trouble seedlings, transplanted onions and bulb onions of any size, and it can cause severe losses in shallots. No one quite knows how the disease spreads, but the fungus can travel at least five yards through the soil in one year by its own efforts. It is normally carried from garden to garden and allotment to allotment on gardening tools and the dirty boots of workers. *Control Measures* A special powder known as Calotox should be applied before sowing or transplanting onions. It is no good making an application once the disease has appeared. One pound of the powder should be dusted along a drill 50 yds long and this equals about 1 heaped tsp. per yd run. Transplanted onion seedlings and shallots may be dipped in a stiff paste made up by stirring 3 lb. Calotox powder in 1 pt water. The shallots should be dipped halfway up and be planted immediately, and the onion seedlings may be dipped up to their first leaves.

Parsnip

CANKER

A very widespread disease. No one knows really whether it originates from any specific parasite or not. It is thought that the trouble originates from some injury. Anyway, the tissue cracks, turns rusty brown and eventually a brown rot may appear. Sometimes this is followed by a wet black rot. *Control Measures* The varieties *Large Guernsey* and *Tender and True* are said to be resistant. *Avon Resister* is almost immune.

No method of control is known.

1

2

3

4

1   *Cockchafer larva – a destructive root feeder*

2   *Cockchafer or 'May Bug', male*

3   *Common earwig, female*

4   *Crane-fly or daddy-long-legs, female*

5

6

7

8

5   *Leatherjacket – larva of crane-fly*

6   *Common millipede*

7   *Common centipede*

8   *Colorado beetle*

Pea

MARSH SPOT

An obscure trouble which is common all over the country. Difficult to see externally, but when the seeds are split open a brown spot will be found in the centre of the seed leaves or cotyledons. The seedlings produced from such seeds are weak and often mutilated. They are frequently branched at, or below ground level. *Control measures* As the cause of Marsh Spot is not known it is difficult to suggest control. It may be that the trouble can be prevented by applying manganese to the soil in the form of magnesium sulphate or borax, or even both. When using either of these, dissolve 1 tsp. in 2 gal. water and apply this over 30 sq. yds.

MILDEW (*Erysiphe polygoni*)

Both the leaves, stems and pods will be attacked and will be found covered with whitish powdery patches. The disease occurs every season, usually towards the end of the summer. It is particularly bad on late varieties. *Control Measures* Dust with a fine sulphur dust early in the morning immediately after the first symptoms have appeared. Dust again a week later, or sooner should it rain in between.

Other diseases which may attack peas are Root Rot, Black Root Rot and Leaf and Pod Spot.

Potato

BLACK LEG (*Erwinia carotovora* subsp, *atroseptica*)

Plants may die before, or soon after they appear above the ground so that 'blanks' occur in the row. The first signs of the disease are seen early in the season, before the haulm meets across the drills.

Attacked plants are often stunted and 'hard', with pale green or yellowish foliage. The leaves are stiff and erect, and their margins roll inwards. The base of the stem below soil level, is black and rotted, but still firm; not all the stems of a plant may be affected. The old seed tuber is invariably completely rotted.

As the season advances the leaves turn brown and the haulm dies.

The affected tubers usually have a dark line around the margin of the rotted tissue. In bad attacks all the tubers decay in the ground; but the disease does not usually advance rapidly. Thus the tubers remain sound for a long time and then decay in storage. Slightly affected tubers may even survive the winter but if planted they produce diseased plants.

Losses may occur during storage as a result of the infection of healthy tubers through contact with the diseased ones. The bacteria enter by way of the breathing pores and, of course, through wounds.

Black leg can be spread by the planting of diseased tubers. Such tubers may be so slightly infected as to appear quite sound, but if used as seed, may produce diseased plants.

Infected tubers on apparently healthy plants result from movement of bacteria through the soil from diseased to healthy potatoes.

The black leg bacteria do not survive in the soil itself in the absence of a potato crop for more than a few weeks. *Control Measures* The tubers of affected plants should be dug up and removed.

Do not use seed from places where soft or hard rot has occurred. Whole tubers of the right size are preferable to cut sets, because the black leg bacteria may be carried on the knife.

No varieties are known to be resistant to this disease, but the disease is worse in some varieties like *Majestic, Arran Pilot* and *Arran Consul* than, for instance, in *King Edward*.

BLIGHT (*Phytophthora infestans*)
One of the commonest potato diseases. The leaves of the potato are attacked first, and irregular dark green spots or blotches appear on them. These soon turn brown or black and become covered with a delicate white mould. In damp, muggy weather the disease spreads rapidly, and in a bad attack the whole of the tops may be killed. The spores fall to the ground and infect the tubers, which develop darker sunken areas on the skin, and the whole potato soon becomes rotten and useless. *Control Measures* Bordeaux Mixture is the usual remedy for blight, though in smoky districts near towns it is advisable to use Burgundy mixture instead, as the acid smoke has an adverse reaction with Bordeaux Mixture. The formulae for both these fungicides will be found in chapter 13. The plants should be sprayed thoroughly with the solution about the end of June, and further applications made at 2–3 week intervals. Alternatively, a copper-lime dust may be used. If a bad attack

occurs, the haulms may be cut off when they die down, or even before. This will to some extent prevent the blight spores from falling onto the soil and being carried down to the tubers.

COMMON SCAB (*Actiomyces scabies*)
This disease causes the familiar brown, corky scabs to appear on the tubers, in consequence of which the potatoes have to be peeled more deeply and there is a lot of waste. The disease is usually more prevalent in district where the soil is gravelly or sandy, or where it is very alkaline owing to large applications of lime, or to the addition of ashes or unbalanced fertilisers. *Control Measures* When planting, the trench should be filled up with grass or lawn mowings. Putting a handful of lawn mowings around each potato is an excellent plan.

WART DISEASE (*Synchytrium endobioticum*)
Wart is a very serious disease, but very few attacks are experienced nowadays as immune varieties are available. If an outbreak does occur it is necessary to notify the Ministry of Agriculture. It first appears round the 'eyes' of the tuber, where small wrinkles or warts appear. These gradually get larger, until the whole tuber may become a blackish-brown spongy mass. *Control Measures* The following is a list of some of the best known varieties which are immune to wart disease: *Arran Pilot, Home Guard, Ulster, Chieftain, Arran Banner, Catriona, Gladstone, Redskin, Di Vernon, Olympic, Ben Lomond, Ulster Ensign, Dunbar Rover, Bally Doon, Duke of Kent, Dunbar Standard, Arran Peak, Arran Consul.*

VIRUS DISEASES
In most parts of England potatoes become unprofitable after being grown for one or two years. This 'running out' as it is called, is due to the rapid increase in virus diseases.

Affected stocks of course give poor yields. When the attack is, say, 20 per cent affected, the yield is much reduced.

A virus is a micro-organism present in the sap of diseased plants. The viruses causing leaf roll and severe mosaic are spread from plant to plant by aphids. When an aphid feeds on an infected plant it picks up some of the virus and then injects it into a healthy plant. The small amount of virus injected multiplies and is carried with the sap throughout the plant, eventually causing recognisable symptoms. The virus then infects the tubers and in this way diseases are perpetuated.

The worst of all the potato virus diseases is leaf roll. Healthy plants that become infected with this disease unfortunately show no symptoms in the first season of infection.

A few weeks after the plant is up, the lower leaves show a rolling upwards and inwards of the margins of their leaflets. As the plant grows, this rolling generally becomes apparent, thus the whole foliage has a rolled appearance (fig. 1).

Besides being rolled, the leaves are generally thicker and drier and more curly than usual. On stunted plants the leaves point upwards. This gives the plant a stiff and gaunt appearance. The whole plant lacks vigour and is usually undersized. Towards the end of the season the lower leaves dry out and turn brown at the margins.

Affected plants produce fewer tubers and these are smaller than usual.

VIRUS Y

Very severe mosaic is caused by a potato virus called Y. It is second to leaf roll in importance. The plants are dwarfed and the leaves often have a roughened surface and are yellow-green in colour. Later on the stems become weak and lie on the ground. The lower leaves then drop easily. The disease is often given the name of the Rugose mosaic. Affected plants give a poor crop of tiny tubers, which reproduce the disease if planted. *How the Virus spreads* Leaf roll and the mosaics are spread by aphids and particularly by the peach-potato aphids (*Myzus persicae*). This over-winters as an egg on peach trees, and sometimes also as wingless aphids on many differing crops in glasshouses and in mild winters out of doors on cabbages, Brussels sprout and kale.

In spring, the winged aphids fly to the potato crop. They alight on the plants and feed on these, often depositing wingless young. If the crop is affected with mosaic, the virus is soon transmitted to healthy plants. There may also be transmission later on in the season by wingless aphids crawling from plant to plant. Winged aphids move most actively when the temperature is high and the wind low. Warm, still weather in spring or summer favours the spread of leaf roll and mosaic.

Fortunately, stocks of potatoes when properly rogued, remain healthy for years in Scotland, Ireland and in cold districts of England and Wales. This is because of the scarcity of aphids in these areas, which keeps disease transmission at a minimum. *How different varieties behave* Some varieties, i.e. *Ulster*

Concord, are very susceptible to leaf roll infection. Others, which include *Arran Pilot* and *Ulster Sceptre,* are susceptible to mosaic. *Pentland Crown,* on the other hand, is resistant to leaf roll and mosaic. *Desirée, Ulster Chieftain* and *Pentland Beauty* are resistant to mosaic, but only slightly resistant to leaf roll.

All gardeners are advised to purchase only certified seed. Health certificates are now issued in England and Wales:

(1) 'S.S.' (Stock Seed) Certificate for seed from crops at least 99.95 per cent true to type, that contain not more than a very small number of virus infected plants per acre.

(2) 'A' Certificate for seed from crops at least 99.5 per cent true to type, that contain not more than about 0.5 per cent of severe virus diseases.

(3) 'H' Certificate for seed from crops at least 99.5 per cent true to type, that contain not more than about 2 per cent of severe virus diseases.

Radish

CLUB ROOT
See **Cabbage**.

Rhubarb

ROT (*Bacterium rhaponticum*)
The leaves gradually turn a puce colour and the bases of the stems become distorted and woollen. The crown of the plant usually goes soft and rotten and the terminal bud may be destroyed. When the disease gets a firm hold only spindly, useless shoots appear. *Control Measures* When purchasing plants, care should be taken not to accept any which show any sign of rot at all, especially around the crown. All infected plants should be removed and burnt together with all refuse around.

Seakale

BLACK ROT (*Pseudomonas campestris*)
A common disease of seakale, particularly where the soil is badly drained or where the subsoil has not been disturbed. Black streaks appear first of all in the roots and finally the whole plant turns black and rots away. *Control Measures* Never plant seakale on land that is not properly drained. Never plant thongs that show any black streaks.

Other diseases which attack seakale are Violet Root Rot and Club Root.

Spinach

DOWNY MILDEW (*Peronospora effusa*)
A very common disease of spinach which sometimes causes serious damage. The leaves may be covered with yellow spots and a violet-grey or grey mould develops on the under-sides of the leaves as well as soon the upper. *Control Measures* See that the land is properly drained, for moist conditions favour the disease. Give the plants a good dusting with a reliable sulphur dust or spray with a 1 in 100 solution of lime-sulphur. On the whole, dusting is preferable if well done.

Turnip

CLUB ROOT AND BLACK LEG

SOFT ROT
See **Celery.**
Other diseases that may attack turnips are Dry Rot, Mildew, Downy Mildew, Leaf Spot and White Blister.

Tomato

LEAF MOULD (*Cladosporium fulvum*)
A very common disease of tomatoes, particularly under glass. Usually occurs in July and August.

The pale grey fungus appears as a mould first of all on the under-side of the leaves in large spots. This fungus changes to tawny olive and finally to purple. The upper surfaces of the leaves turn pale yellow and then reddish brown. The leaves next become brown and brittle and finally die. The fungus spreads most rapidly under humid conditions. *Control Measures* Fortunately, there are tomato varieties available which are immune from this disease. Thus gardeners who have been troubled with Cladosporium in the past should grow such varieties as *Seville Cross, Eurocross B, Amberley Cross* and *Grenadier.*

STREAK OR STRIPE
The disease may be recognised by the long brown stripes

which appear on the stems and by the mottling and final shrivelling of the leaves. Sunken irregularly shaped brown blotches will appear also on the fruits.

This disease which should now be called streak, for the old term 'stripe' has been reserved for the attack made by the *Baccillus lathyri,* is undoubtedly a virus. There are various types of viruses but at the present time little is known about them. *Control Measures* Affected leaves may be cut off with the blade of a knife that has been disinfected by dipping it in a 2 per cent solution of formaldehyde. This will prevent the virus being transmitted to other plants.

Wood ashes should be applied to the ground before planting the tomatoes at 8 oz to the sq. yd.

SLEEPY DISEASE OR WILT (*Fusarium* or *Verticillium*)
The sleepy disease of tomatoes may either be caused by a fusarium or a verticillium. The roots are invaded by the fungi and the plant wilts badly in consequence.

In the case of the fusarium, the trouble is largely due to high temperatures and consequently is seldom seen in this country. At any rate, it only occurs in the height of summer.

In the case of verticillium it usually appears about the middle of April and goes on, generally with increasing intensity, until the second or third week of May. Then it will disappear, only to reappear again in about the middle of September.

It is affected by the temperature of the soil and the air. In low temperatures, affected plants will wilt suddenly and die quickly. If the temperature is moderately high the foliage does not wilt, but yellow patches appear on the leaves which slowly shrivel from the base of the plant upwards. *Control Measures* In the case of the Fusarium wilt, control can usually be secured if the temperature is reduced immediately.

In the case of the Verticillium wilt the temperature in the greenhouse should be raised to 77°F. A light dressing of whitening should be sprayed on the outside of the glass, and as little water as possible should be given to the roots. It is curious that watering should aggravate wilting, but it does. The plants, however, should be syringed overhead, as this helps them to recover.

It is a good plan also, to earth up the soil to the plants and then they make fresh roots above the original diseased ones.

DAMPING-OFF OR FOOT ROT (*Phytophthora cryptogea, prasitica,* or *Corticum solani,* etc.)
Tomato seedlings are attacked, the stems rotting off at, or above soil level. The plants then topple over. The trouble is commonly known as Damping-off. *Control Measures* Prevent excessive moisture in the seed boxes or pots. Keep the temperature as low as possible and avoid overcrowding.

Check the spread of the disease by watering with Cheshunt Compound. (For formula see chapter 13.)

BLIGHT (*Phytophthora infestans*)
This is a common disease of tomatoes grown in the open, especially during the months of July and August if the season is wet. The foliage will become affected, and blackish purple spots edged with a white down will show itself. The fruits will be covered with sunken spots of a dark brown or leaden colour. Later they may be involved in a wet or dry rot. *Control Measures* Spray with a Bordeaux mixture immediately the disease is detected as advised for Potato. Any plants that are seriously attacked should be pulled up and burnt. Alternatively, a copper white oil emulsion spray may be used.

BUCK-EYE ROT (*Phytophthora parasitica*)
In the early part of the year coloured patches will appear on the fruits on the bottom trusses. These will vary from grey to brown and will usually take the form of concentric rings. The trouble starts at the blossom end of the fruit as a rule. *Control Measures* Everything must be done to prevent soil from being splashed on to the fruit during watering, so mulch the ground with straw or peat.

Spray the soil and lower parts of the plant with Cheshunt Compound. (For formula see chapter 13.)

Remove all diseased fruits and burn them. Cut off the lower leaves and so help to keep the fruit dry and allow good circulation of air.

BLOSSOM END ROT (a functional disorder)
No one quite knows what 'parasite', if any, causes this disease. It is probably just a sudden shortage of moisture. Usually it appears as a patch of dark green colour near the exposed end of a fruit. This may look water-soaked to start with but eventually becomes black and leathery.

More prevalent where plants have been over-watered or

where they have suddenly had a check in their water supply. The digging in of too much stable manure or using too much nitrogen in some chemical form usually favours the development of the trouble. *Control Measures* All watering done to tomatoes must be regular but never excessive. Drainage should be perfect.

Lime seems to have some effect in neutralising the effect of heavy watering. It may be applied in the form of hydrated lime at 4–5 oz to the sq. yd.

ROOT ROT (*Colletotrichum altramentarium*)
Usually occurs in June and July when the temperature of the soil is high. As a rule, however, it is not seen till about the middle of August. The lower leaves turn yellow and wither, and death may follow. The trouble usually develops more quickly when the soil is rich in organic matter for the fungus thrives on such material. *Control Measures* Sterilise soil known to be contaminated with this fungus. (See chapter 12.) Water the soil around the plants with a solution of Cheshunt Compound. (For formula, see Chapter 13.)
Other diseases which may attack tomatoes are Mosaic (see 'The Virus Problem', chapter 4.) Spotted Wilt (see chapter 4) and Grey Mould.

7 The pests of flowers

There are a number of pests which attack flowering plants as a whole, just in the same way that there are pests which attack plants generally as described in chapter 3. Perhaps the six main general pests of garden plants are capsid bugs, tarnished plant bugs, cuckoo spit, angle shades moth caterpillars, swift moth caterpillars and tortrix moth caterpillars.

CAPSID BUG (*Lygus pabulinus*)
This pest is fully described in chapter 9. It feeds on a wide range of plants, including shrubs, herbaceous plants, annuals and, of course, weeds. The bug is bright green and when an adult can fly. *Control Measures* The best method of control is to spray with nicotine and soft soap. (For formula, see chapter 13.) Those who dislike using nicotine may use pyrethum instead.

TARNISHED PLANT BUG (*Lygus pratensis*)
This is similar to the capsid bug already mentioned, only it is, as its name suggests, browny green mottled with reddish brown. It is a very serious pest to chrysanthemums and other herbaceous plants, particularly zinnia, dahlia and delphinium. It spoils the foliage, malforms and may ruin the flowers. The adult is $\frac{1}{4}$ in. long and may fly from plant to plant. When young it moves about very quickly. In a bad attack the shoots will be malformed and stunted, and the buds go blind. *Control Measures* see Capsid Bug.

CUCKOO SPIT (*Philaenus spumarius*) (*Frog hopper*)
Most people recognise the spittle-like deposit on plants. Inside will be found a green bug, sucking the sap and causing the shoots to wilt. It is a particularly bad pest of lavender, coreopsis, geum, phlox and solidago. *Control Measures* Spray with nicotine and soft soap (for formula see chapter 13); with liquid derris or with a good pyrethrum extract such as Pysect.

ANGLE SHADES MOTH CATERPILLAR (*Phlogophora meticulosa*)
This moth is rather interesting, for when it is resting on a tree

trunk or on herbage it folds its wings into its body and looks like a crumpled decaying leaf.

The young caterpillars are olive green or brownish in colour and feed on the leaves of flower buds and on open blossoms. They are very fond of winter-flowering iris, gladiolus, dahlia, hollyhock, primula, wallflower, St Brigid anemone, and many herbaceous plants. Under glass they attack chrysanthemum, geranium, pelargonium, and cineraria, and may do untold damage to violets in frames. *Control Measures* Spray directly the caterpillars are seen, and even before, with liquid derris, giving the plants a thorough soaking.

SWIFT MOTH CATERPILLARS (*Hepialus* spp)
The white active larvae of the moths live in the soil and may feed on herbaceous plants, strawberries, vegetable crops, bulbs, corms, tubers and rhizomes. They are whitish with a reddish-brown head and a number of dark dots along the body. They may feed for two years.

They can do a tremendous amount of harm to delphinium, lupin, rudbeckia and to dahlia, gladiolus and iris. *Control Measures* Hoe the ground regularly and fork in very lightly crude naphthalene at the rate of 3 oz. per sq. yd during soil preparation.

TORTRIX MOTH CATERPILLARS (*Cephasia* spp)
Various tortrix moth caterpillars are known as 'leaf-tyers' and injure various herbaceous plants, especially phlox, helenium, solidago and rudbeckia. The little caterpillars draw together two or three leaves, fastening them with silken threads. They may be olive or greyish green and they usually appear in May or June. These caterpillars often feed on the flowers of members of the chrysanthemum family. *Control Measures* Spray liquid pyrethrum as an emulsion, usual strength, or use Pysect. Treat in good time before the larvae have had time to become inaccessible. Hand picking can be done in the advanced stages of an attack.

Auricula

ROOT APHIS (*Pentaphis auriculae*)
The foliage yellows and wilts and around the collar – that is, the part where the stem joins the root – the root aphids will be found. They are pale green or white covered with white mealy

threads. *Control Measures* Lift the plants, wash the roots in nicotine and soft soap (usual formula). Dip the whole plant in this solution for two minutes.

Remove soil from round about attacked plants and replace with sterilised compost.

If it is impossible to lift the plants, water the soil, giving it a thorough soaking with a solution of nicotine and water.

Formula: 1 oz. nicotine and 5 gal. water.

Carnation

APHIS
See p. 18.

RED SPIDER
See p. 35.

SLUGS
See p. 25.

Chrysanthemum

APHIDS, EARWIGS and EELWORM
See pp. 18, 21 and 22.

CAPSID BUGS
See chapter 9.

Chrysanthemums are also liable to attack by both the midge, which can usually be controlled by thorough ventilation and spraying; and the leaf miner which can also be largely controlled by the use of insecticide.

Cornflower

APHIDS
See chapter 3, p. 18.

Dahlia

May be attacked by eelworms, earwigs, caterpillars and capsids. For control see chapter 3 and beginning of this chapter.

Chrysanthemum leaf miner

Iris

The irises may be damaged by slugs, snails, eelworms and caterpillars.

SAWFLY (*Rhadinoceroea micans*)
The little caterpillars of this sawfly eat large pieces out of the edges of the leaves in June and July. *Control Measures* Spray with a pyrethrum or derris wash, adding 2 oz. gelatine to every 10 gal. mixed wash to prevent it being washed off by rain.

Lupin

WEEVIL (*Sitona lineata*)
A grey weevil which eats crescent-shaped pieces out of the leaves. Control Measures Dust with derris at night time. Give young seedlings a dressing of nitrate of soda at 1 oz. to the sq. yd.

Narcissus

NARCISSUS FLIES (*Meroden equestris* and *Eumerus* spp)
The fly lays its eggs on the neck of the bulbs in May. Small maggots emerge and burrow down to the centre of the bulbs. The tips of the leaves turn yellow and cease to grow. When bulbs are cut open grubs will be found in the centre. *Control Measures* Sterilise bulbs in warm water as advised in chapter 12.

The maggots of the narcissus flies are easily killed by the hot-water treatment. All bulbs can be treated after they are lifted; if this is done by hot-water treatment, any maggots in the bulbs will be killed. Fly maggots can be killed by 1 hour's treatment at 110°F or 112°F.

Derris dust should be applied thickly on the remains of the foliage, and the hole in the soil above the bulb. This should be done in May–June and, if necessary, repeated in July.

Spray on warm sunny days at 11 a.m. when flies are on the wing. Spray ground, banks, hedges, etc.

Never plant soft bulbs. Lift bulbs every two or three years.

Phlox

EELWORM *Control Measures* Take root cuttings from well washed roots only, as the eelworm lives in the stem and leaves. Preferably do the washing under a running tap.

Primula

ROOT APHIS
See **Auricula**

Rose

APHIDS
See p. 18.

RED BUD BURER
Midge appears mid July to mid August and lays eggs in
wounds made during budding. *Control Measures* Smear buds
and raffia with vaseline directly after budding.

CATERPILLARS and MAGGOTS
The larvae of many moths attack the leaves and buds of roses.
Control Measures Spray with nicotine and soft soap or liquid
derris.

SAWFLIES
Various sawflies attack rose leaves, some eating them and
boring into the stems; some, like the slug worms, skeletonising
the leaves and feeding on the under surface; and others by
rolling up the leaves tightly. *Control Measures* Spray with
arsenate of lead (for formula see chapter 15) at the end of
May.

Spray again with nicotine and soft soap in June. Hand pick
and burn all rolled leaves and cut off and burn tunnelled
branches.

SCALE (*Diaspis rosae*)
The stems of the bushes become covered with round, flat
whitish scales. *Control Measures* Pysect spray is effective and is
preferable to derris dust as the latter leaves a slight deposit on
the foliage.

WEEVIL (*Otiorrhynchus singularis*)
A clay-covered weevil which is particularly destructive to
rambler roses in spring and early summer. It will eat the lower
buds and girdle the stems. *Control Measures* Place a white cloth
under the attacked bush after dark. Shake the bush and direct
a bright light on to it. The weevils then fall off and can be
collected and burnt. The light should be maintained and not
just flashed.

Sweet Pea

APHIDS
See p. 18.

Tulip

APHIDS
See p. 18.

Violet

Treat very much in the same way as strawberries for both are
attacked by aphides and eelworms.

RED SPIDER (*Tetranychus telarius*)
One of the worst pests of violets. There is one variety which
seems to be resistant, that is *Governor Herrick*. *Control Measures*
Keep the soil in the frames moist. Syringe the plants daily if
enclosed. Dry conditions encourage red spiders. Spray with
clean water using 100 lb. pressure in cases of slight attacks,
and in bad cases strip the whole of the infected plants.

Petroleum sprays have proved effective if a good sousing is
given. A second spraying is, however, necessary in 12 days.

8 The diseases of flowers

Unfortunately, there are a large number of diseases which attack garden flowers, many of which, like Mildew, are quite common. It has not been possible to deal with every fungus disease in detail, but all the more important 'troubles' are dealt with.

In obvious cases where, for instance, the disease is not dealt with under the particular flower concerned, the gardener should adopt the method of digging up the plant and burning it in order to prevent the spread of the trouble. It must be remembered, too, that fungus diseases are usually controlled either by sulphur in some form, i.e. lime-sulphur, liver of sulphur, sulphur dust, or with copper in some form, usually Bordeaux mixture, Burgundy mixture, colloidal copper, and so on.

In order that the remedy may be applied immediately, the garden medicine chest should be kept stocked with the fungicides needed.

Colloidal copper and colloidal sulphur are very useful to have, for, on the whole, they are safer to use than any of the other fungicides mentioned. Further, they have an advantage with flower plants in that they don't 'spot' or mark the leaves. Zinc fungicides for mildew are good, non-toxic, Zinab is one of these.

Antirrhinum

LEAF SPOT (*Septoria antirrhinum*)
This fungus attacks the leaves and stems of the plants causing pale brown or whitish spots. *Control Measures* Spray with potassium sulphide or Bordeaux mixture.

RUST (*Puccinia antirrhinum*)
A prevalent disease of antirrhinum for the past ten years. Recognised by rusty-brown patches on the under sides of the leaves. If severely attacked the plants wither and die. The

disease spreads rapidly from plant to plant. *Control Measures* Avoid overcrowding the plants – give ample room between them for the air and light to get in. Stagnant, water-laden air encourages the disease. See that the beds are well drained, and if necessary to water, do this in the morning, rather than in the evening, so that surplus water is not left lying about overnight. Avoid watering the foliage.

Dust with sulphur or spray with one of the sulphur sprays at weekly intervals, to prevent and control the disease.

Arabis

WHITE RUST (*Cystopus candidus*)
This appears on the leaf as shining raised white patches. Rarely severe enough to cause serious damage. *Control Measures* Dust with flowers of sulphur. If on small scale remove diseased flowers and leaves and burn.

GREY MOULD (*Peronospora parasitica*)
This disease appears in patches on the leaves. The spots are first pale in colour and then turn brown, having a greyish-white powdery fungus on them. *Control Measures* See Rust above.

Aster, Michaelmas Daisy

WILT (*Verticillium vilmorinii*)
This disease enters through a damaged portion of the plant and shows as a yellow mottling of the lower leaves in the summer. This is followed by a complete browning of the leaves and towards the end of the summer the whole shoot will wilt. *Control Measures* Do not propagate by division of diseased plants – but select healthy shoots and take cuttings from them.

STEM ROT (*Fusarium* spp)
The leaves and flowers hang down and become yellow-green and later brown, and die off. The stem will be black in colour. *Control Measures* Do not over-manure the border and give occasional dressings of lime at 5–6 oz. per sq. yd. Remove and burn attacked plants. The variety *American Beauty* is resistant to this disease.

YELLOW VIRUS DISEASE
See disorders caused by viruses, chapter 4.

Carnation

RUST (*Uromyces dianthi*)
This can be a serious disease of carnations, especially in a wet season. Yellowish brown cushions appear on the leaves and they may be killed. *Control Measures* Pick off infected leaves. Have plants in a well-drained sunny spot. Do not splash leaves when watering. Spray with colloidal copper, or Bordeaux mixture.

LEAF SPOT (*Septoria dianthi*)
Leaf spots caused by various fungi are found on the leaves of the carnations. Some may have black centres. *Control Measures* Bouisol spray as recommended for Rust.

LEAF ROT (*Heteropatella dianthi*)
Border carnations are often attacked, the base of the leaves rotting and dying off. *Control Measures* Destroy all susceptible varieties.

DIE BACK and WILT (*Fusarium* spp)
This disease is more prevalent under glass than in the garden. *Control Measures* Do not grow carnations in the same spot. Propagate from healthy plants.

Chrysanthemum

MILDEW (*Oidium chrysanthemi*)
White powdery patches may be seen towards the end of the season on the leaves, both upper and lower surfaces. *Control Measures* Spray with a colloidal sulphur or use Karothane wash when the disease is first noticed.

RUST (*Puccinia chrysanthemi*)
Most varieties of chrysanthemum are attacked by this disease. Red rusty spots are seen on the under surfaces of the leaves. Usually worse in dry seasons and with excessively manured plants. *Control Measures* Watch out for the rusty patches and spray at once with colloidal copper, or Bordeaux mixture. Remove and burn leaves in autumn. Plant least susceptible varieties.

MOSAIC
See **Viruses,**

DRY ROT
Dry, unsuitable storage places seem to encourage this trouble.
Control Measures Dig up tubers before the first frost. Stand
upside down for several days to drain thoroughly. Protect from
frost in airy cool storage place. Dust tubers with equal quantity of sulphur and lime when storing. Disinfect storage place
with formaldehyde before the tubers go into position. Leave
for two or three days afterwards to allow the fumes to disperse.

Delphinium

BACTERIAL SPOT (*Bacterium delphinii*)
Deep, black, irregularly shaped spots appear on both sides of
the leaves and may spread to the stalks and blossoms. Seeds
may also be infected. *Control Measures* Collect and burn all diseased foliage. Spray repeatedly with colloidal copper or
Bordeaux mixture. In severe attacks cut down plants and
burn.

MILDEW (*Erysiphe polygoni*)
A white flour-like dust is found on the leaves and stalks and
blossoms. The leaves die off prematurely and the buds dry up.
In severe attacks the whole plant is stunted. *Control Measures*
Avoid over-manuring with nitrogenous matter. Give plenty of
space between the plants. Spray with colloidal copper or
Bordeaux mixture in warm sunny weather.

STALK AND BULB ROT (*Sclerotinia sclerotiorum*)
See **Aquilegia.**

Erica (Heath)

MILDEW (*Oidium* sp)
The leaves and young shoots become covered with a white
powdery mildew. *Control Measures* Dust with a fine sulphur
dust or use a Karathane spray.

Geranium, zonal pelargonium

STEM ROT (*Fusarium pelargonii*)
The attacked stem becomes black and decays. The leaves turn
sickly yellow. Pale spots appear on diseased part of stem.
Control Measures Destroy plants by burning.

BACTERIAL LEAF SPOT (*Bacterium pelargonii*)
First shows as a water-soaked dot. Later becomes well defined.
Irregular in shape, sometimes round and brown in colour.
Leaves turn first yellow, then brown and finally red. *Control
Measures* Plant out plants in open airy situation, leaving plenty
of space between them. Hand pick diseased leaves and flowers
and burn them.
   Spray stock and plants with a good Bordeaux mixture.

GREY MOULD (*Botrytis cinerea Auct.*)
The flowers fade and die prematurely and a grey mould
appears. The fungus spreads from the petals to the leaves.
Control Measures As for Leaf Spot.

LEAF SPOT (*Cercospora Brunkii*)
Round spots light brown or brick red in colour are found on
the leaves. These may be slightly raised and may join together
till they cover most of the leaf surface. *Control Measures* See
Bacterial Leaf Spot above.

BLACK LEG (*Pythium* spp)
A common disease of cuttings and young plants. Stem and leaf
stalk become black and shrivelled. The rot starts at the base of
the stem. *Control Measures* Be careful not to over-water. Shade if
sun is very bright. Maintain even temperature with adequate
ventilation. Water with Cheshunt Compound for formula, see
chapter 15).

Gladiolus

BASE DECAY (*Bacterium marginatum*)
Reddish-brown raised spots appear on the leaves towards the
base. These spots increase in size and may become black and
pitted. A wet rot may develop inside and the bases of the leaves
and stalks thus be destroyed. *Control Measures* Destroy all diseased leaves by burning. Do not plant corms in heavy wet soil.
Only store healthy corms.

SMUT (*Tubercinia gladioli*)
Black cushions appear on the corms, leaves and stalks. The
corms become completely destroyed. *Control Measures* Remove
and burn infected plants. Dig the ground deeply. Lime the soil
heavily, say garden lime at $\frac{1}{2}$ lb. to the sq. yd.

DRY ROT (*Sclerotium gladioli*)
When the corm is split dry sunken spots will be found, reddish brown in colour. As the plant grows in the spring the leaves become yellow and then turn brown. The stem will decay at soil level and the leaves fall earlier.

Infection invariably is caused through the soil. *Control Measures* Buy good clean corms. Remove scales so as to look for sunken spots.

HARD ROT (*Septoria gladioli*)
The leaves are attacked, yellow patches appearing which later turn brown. Hard dark spots are produced on the corms. The fungus may live in the soil for four years. *Control Measures* Do not plant in infected soil. Reject infected corms. Other diseases which may attack gladioli are Grey Bulb Rot (see **Tulip**) Penicillium Rot and Fusarium Bulb Rot.

Hollyhock

RUST (*Puccinia malvacearum*)
Discoloured small spots will be found on the upper surfaces of leaves. Reddish-brown rusty cushions will be seen on the lower surfaces. These become dark brown later. *Control Measures* It is important to raise new plants every year for young plants are seldom attacked.

Should seedlings be attacked, spray with colloidal copper.

Iris

RHIZOME ROT (*Pseudomonas iridis*)
The rhizomous roots become soft, putrid smelling masses. The base of the leaves rot away. *Control Measures* Do not apply lime as an alkaline soil encourages the trouble. Take up all diseased portions and burn them. Cut out diseased portions from slightly attacked rhizomes and wash thoroughly in a 2 per cent solution of formaldehyde. Replant in new or sterilised soil.

IRIS SCORCH
The leaves look as if they had been on a bonfire. Is probably another form of rot and should be treated in a similar manner.

LEAF SPOT (*Heterosporium gracile*)
Yellowish brown spots, stripes and marks appear on the leaves early in the autumn. *Control Measures* Spray the leaves with

lime-sulphur, 1 pint to 100 pts water. three or four times during the summer. Cut off infected portions of leaves when seen in the autumn, and burn them.

Lily

LEAF SPOT (*Botrytis cinerea*)
Reddish-brown spots appear on the leaves. These may enlarge and cover the whole surface. The leaves will die, the stem may dry up and the flowers may be distorted. The trouble spreads rapidly.

Madonna lilies and its hybrids are the most susceptible. *Control Measures* Spray with colloidal sulphur two or three times at weekly intervals. Bordeaux mixture is effective but is inclined to mark the foliage.

In severe cases give the surface of the soil a good soaking with Bordeaux mixture and spray the young growths when they first appear in the spring.

Plant bulbs in an open sunny position on well-drained soil. A stagnant atmosphere is conducive to the disease.

MOSAIC
The leaves become mottled and distorted and the petals usually remain closed. *Control Measures* No known cure. Infected plants should be taken up and burnt. As aphids are probably the carriers of this disease, see that they are kept down with nicotine and soft soap.

Lupin

ROOT ROT (*Thielaviopsis basicola*)
Attacks the roots of the plants turning them black. From these blackened portions a white fungus will be found growing. *Control Measures* Do not plant lupins on the same ground for four years and do not add lime to the soil as this seems to encourage disease.

Narcissus

GREY BULB ROT (*Sclerotium tuliparum*)
Gaps may be noticed, or only weak shoots appear. When bulbs are dug up they will be found to be rotten. *Control Measures* Burn diseased bulbs. Do not plant in the same spot for four years.

Water soil thoroughly with 2 per cent solution of for-maldehyde.

YELLOW STRIPE (*Ramularia narcissi*)
Yellowish light-green streaks will be found on the leaves and flower stems and in bad cases even on the flowers themselves. The stripes vary according to the variety attacked. In the case of *King Alfred* and *Victoria,* for instance, it is much more virulent than in the case of *Sir Watkin* and *Golden Spur.*

In bad cases the leaves become distorted and the bulbs blind. *Control Measures* Remove and burn diseased bulbs directly they are detected. A sharp look-out should be kept when they are 6 in. high.

Paeony

BOTRYTIS (*Botrytis paeoniae*)
The shoots are attacked above soil level. They wilt and turn brown. Later the fully developed leaves may be attacked. The roots will rot but rarely does the plant die. *Control Measures* Cut off affected leaves and burn them. Each winter cut down the foliage and burn. Never plant on infected soil.

Dust with a good copper-lime dust immediately the trouble is seen.

ROOT GALL See **Dahlia,** Crown Gall.

Rose

BLACK SPOT (*Diplocarpon rosae*)
Purplish-black irregular shaped spots appear on the leaves and young stems. The whole bush may lose its leaves. *Control Measures* Spray with Maneb or colloidal copper directly the spots are seen. Repeat the spray in fourteen days. Next season spray as soon as the young leaves are well developed. Mulch the beds with plenty of compost or sedge peat, moisten to prevent the spores blowing up from the soil. Pick off the badly infected leaves and compost them. Some have used an infusion of elderberry leaves as a spray with great success.

MILDEW (*Sphaerotheca pannosa*)
The white powdery mildew will be found on the leaves, stems and even on the thorns. The flower buds may be attacked and in bad cases the leaves will fall. The disease is always more

acute in a dry summer. The two most susceptible varieties are *Crimson Rambler* and *Dorothy Perkins*. *Control Measures* Spray with colloidal sulphur.

See that the soil gets a good dressing of wood ashes at 6 ozs to the sq. yd.

RUST (*Phragmidium Mucronatum*)
Orange spots appear on the under surface of the leaves. In severe attacks many of the leaves will fall. If the disease is allowed to establish itself, the bush usually dies. *Control Measures* Cut out diseased stems. Spray the leaves with colloidal copper or Bordeaux mixture directly the disease is seen, and again ten days later.

SMUT (*Ustilago vaillantii*)
The plants are attacked in their seedling stages and never recover. The only thing to do is to destroy the plants.

Snowdrop

GREY MOULD (*Botrytis galanthina*)
The leaves and bulbs become covered with a grey mould. Rot sets in. *Control Measures* Dig up and burn affected bulbs, being careful to remove soil near by also, as this will also be infected with the fungus.

Sweet Pea

STEM ROT (*Fusarium* spp)
This disease is most severe in wet seasons. The lower part of the stem turns brown and rots at soil level. The leaves turn yellow and wilt and the whole plant flags. *Control Measures* Avoid planting on ground known to be infected with this disease. Take particular care in the wetter parts of England. Sterilise soil before planting by giving a thorough soaking with 2 per cent solution of formaldehyde. Do not plant in the treated ground for three weeks.

STREAK
It is sometimes said that this disorder is due to a virus and other times that it is due to *Bacillus lathyri*.

Long brown streaks will be found on the stem and the foliage will be discoloured also. The whole plant looks sickly and very few flowers are produced. *Control Measures* See that the soil is well fed with wood ashes. Work this in at 6 oz to the sq. yd 10 days or so before planting. Where wood ashes are not obtainable, use finely divided bracken ashes, at ½ lb. to the sq. yd. Where bracken is available compost it specially for sweet peas. This is well worth while doing.

Sweet William

RUST (*Puccinia Lychnidearum*)
Reddish-brown spots appear on the leaves, chiefly on the underside. *Control Measures* Spray with colloidal copper or Bordeaux mixture. The dark red flowered varieties seem to be resistant.

Tulip

FIRE (*Botrytis tulipae*)
A common disease of tulips. Scorched spots will be seen, brownish grey in colour, on the leaves and stems, and pitted spots will appear on the flowers. *Control Measures* Sterilise affected bulbs with formaldehyde. Immerse for 15 minutes in a 0.5 per cent solution.

Dust the tulips immediately they come through the ground with copper-lime dust. Dust again 10 days later and if the weather should be wet, again ten days after that.

SHANKING (*Phytophora cryptogea*)
The base of the stem is attacked, the plant wilts and falls over and the blossom buds die out in consequence. *Control Measures* Sterilise the soil (see chapter 12). Keep plants growing healthily by regular hoeing.

William Copeland is the most susceptible variety.

BREAKING
The plant loses vigour and produces small blooms, if any. The foliage is usually mottled. The bloom will be streaked and speckled.

The trouble is undoubtedly caused by a virus, spread in all probability by aphids which live in the bulb and stem. *Control Measures* Keep down insect pests, particularly aphids, by spraying regularly with nicotine and soft soap or liquid derris.

GREY BULB ROT
See **Narcissus.**

Wallflower
CLUB ROOT see p. 31.

9 The pests of fruit

Unfortunately, there are a very large number of pests which attack fruit trees and bushes, and whole books have been written on the subject. It would be impossible in a manual of this kind to deal with every single insect pest which might damage the various fruits grown in this country, but in this chapter will be found those which are most common as well as those which do the greatest amount of harm.

WINTER WASHING
Ever since tar distillate washes were introduced in the early 1920s, the author has used them to clean up the branches of fruit trees and bushes as well as to kill the eggs of many pests laid on the barks. In the late 1950s it was discovered that in killing the eggs of pests that the predators were killed also and further, that the red spider increased enormously.

As a result, it was decided at the experimental orchards of the International Association of Organic Growers (The GGA) to cease using a tar oil and to apply instead, a white petroleum oil in February, which eliminated the red spiders and cleaned the trees also.

DNOC (Dinitro-ortho-Cresol) suspended in a white oil is used at the strength of 1 in 25 i.e. 1 pt. in 25 pts. of water, gives good control of aphides.

Apple

1 BEETLES

APPLE FRUIT RHYNCHITES (*Rhynchites aequatus*)
More common in the south of England than in the north. The weevil is brownish-red and $\frac{1}{5}$ in. long. Attacks fruits fortnight after petal-fall and goes on doing so till July. Damage done is similar to that made by pushing the point of a lead pencil into the side of the fruit. Hundreds of holes may appear on one apple. *Control Measures* Dust with derris dust on the first warm, sunny day after petal-fall, to destroy the beetle. Using a nicotine plus derris spray for apply sawfly will control rhynchites also.

APPLE TWIG CUTTER (*Rhynchites caeruleus*)
This weevil is of a beautiful blue colour and $\frac{1}{6}$ in. long. It is
more common in the south than in the north. It lays its eggs in
the young shoots cutting them off just below where the eggs
are deposited. The shoots then either fall off, or wither and die.
Control Measures Dust the trees with derris dust about ten days
after petal-fall to destroy the beetle. Give a good application
on a sunny, warm day.

APPLE BLOSSOM WEEVIL
The blossoms when attacked by the weevils do not expand,
and remain brown in colour. In this stage they are usually
called capped blossoms. If the brown cap formed by the dead
petals is pulled off, a whitish grub or a pale yellow chrysalis
will be found inside.
    The weevil itself has a V-shaped white mark on its back and
a grey background. It is not more than $\frac{1}{6}$ in. long. It deposits an
egg in the flower truss before the blossom opens. The grubs
soon hatch out and feed on the stamens. Hundreds of blossoms
may be ruined in this way. *Control Measures* As it becomes
active in March, an insecticide which will rest on the blossom
buds just before they open is desirable. Again there is only
derris and its short-lived potency is a handicap. If a winter
wash is permissible, then a DNOC type should be applied in
March and be followed by derris dust while the buds are still
sticky. This should be repeated a week later and again a week
after that.

2   CATERPILLAR PESTS

LEOPARD MOTH (*Zeuzera pyrina*)
The caterpillar of this moth bores into the limbs of apple trees,
usually confining its activities to trees of 6–10 years in age. Its
presence can usually be determined by sawdust being seen on
the ground below the place of entry of the caterpillar. When
the attack first starts the caterpillar is very small, but when
fully grown it is often two inches in length, yellowish white
with a brown head, marked with black spots. *Control Measures*
If a branch is attacked, saw it off, but if the main trunk is
attacked it is possible to poke a piece of wire up the hole and
hook the caterpillar out. When this is not possible, a small
piece of sodium cyanide should be pushed into the burrow, the
entrance hole being plugged up with clay or plasticine.

Lackey moth egg band (Plant Protection)

LACKEY MOTH (*Malacosoma neustria*)
This is a common pest in the south but rare in the north. Some years it reaches epidemic proportions.

In the winter the egg-bands of this moth will be found laid in a ring completely encircling a spur or twig. This ring consists of eggs stuck together. In the spring these eggs hatch out, and the little caterpillars make silk tents in the crutches of branches. These are very conspicuous early in June. The caterpillars are blue grey in colour with white and reddish-yellow stripes on their backs and sides. They soon defoliate a tree completely and then they move off to another tree. They are usually fully fed early in June and then they spin a silken cocoon either between the leaves or attached to the bark. These have even been found in the grass under the tree. *Control Measures* Use Dinitro-ortho-cresol at $7\frac{1}{2}$ per cent about mid-March. The egg-bands, however, may be cut off during pruning and be burnt. When the nests are seen in May and June these should be removed while the caterpillars are small. When beyond this stage kill by pyrethrum.

VAPOURER MOTH (*Orgyia antiqua*)

The eggs are found in the winter in a mass consisting of about two hundred eggs attached to an empty cocoon. They are usually yellowish brown or reddish grey in colour. The caterpillars hatch out in May and June and feed on the leaves. They are very pretty and have four large yellow tufts of hairs on their backs. *Control Measures* Collect the egg masses in the winter during pruning.

Spray with a DNC wash in February using a $7\frac{1}{2}$ per cent solution.

When caterpillars are present, spray with a derris wash. (For formula, see chapter 13.)

WINTER MOTH (*Operophtera brumata*) MARCH MOTH (*Alsophile aescularia*) MOTTLED UMBER MOTH (*Erannis defoliaria*)

These three moths have been classified together because the damage they do is so similar. The control measures are the same in each case.

The caterpillars of this group are leaf-eating and fruit-eating and are known commonly as loopers, because when they move from place to place they form a half loop in doing so, having only legs in the forefront of their bodies and in the rear.

The female winter moth is wingless and has to crawl up the trunk of the tree to lay her eggs which she does on the spurs and in wounds and cracks in the stems. The caterpillars hatch out in March and April and start feeding on the buds directly they open. They will often defoliate a whole tree. The caterpillar, when mature, is green with palish lines along its body. By the second week in June it is fully fed, and then falls to the ground, turning into a chrysalis four inches below the surface

Winter moth caterpillars on apple shoot (Plant Protection)

of the soil. *Control Measures* Bands of special tree-banding grease may be put straight on to the tree trunks, 3–4 ins. wide. They should be placed as high as possible up the stems of bush trees. The application should be made before the end of October, and from time to time the grease should be 'combed' to remove any leaves or other matter which may have stuck to it.

Spray with DNC in late February.

Should the caterpillars appear in the spring, because grease-banding has been neglected, they may be killed by spraying with pyrethrum. This may be added to the line-sulphur wash if necessary (for formula, see chapter 13).

CODLING MOTH (*Cydia pomonella*) also known as *Ernarmonis pomonella*

The codling moth is an important pest. It causes the maggot or worm which ruins the young fruits. Sometimes it attacks pears, as well as plums, damsons and walnuts.

If an attacked apple is cut open and a pale pinkish caterpillar with a brown head, covered with a few scattered hairs is found inside, this is the maggot of the codling moth. It is usually not more than $\frac{1}{2}$ in. long.

Do not mistake these grubs for the maggots of the apple sawfly. The sawfly maggots emit a very repugnant odour, whereas the codling moth maggots do not. The sawfly caterpillars, too, have usually left the fruit before a codling attack

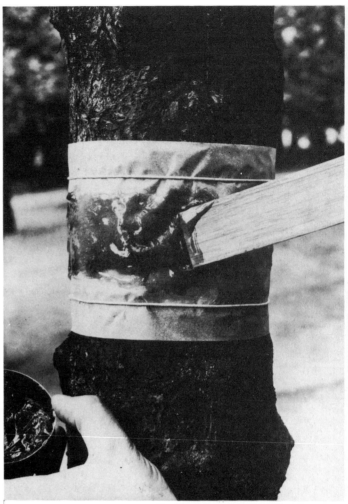

Greasebanding fruit trees with 'Stictite' tree banding, for the prevention of winter moth caterpillar (Plant Protection)

starts. The grubs of the codling are usually to be found in July and August.

Sometimes a second brood occurs, but this is not common in this country.

If the trees are banded in July with sacking, or with corrugated cardboard strips – with the corrugation downwards – the caterpillars will prepare to hibernate in these bands, which

9

10

11

12

9   *White aphids on beech leaf*

10   *Hover fly, female*

11   *Violet ground beetle. A useful insect in the garden*

12   *Tomato moth* (Lacanobia oleracea)

13

14

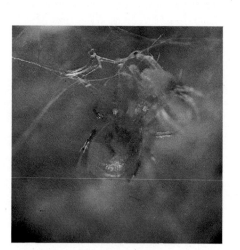

15

16

13   *Tomato moth* (Lacanobia oleracea) *caterpillar*

14   *Adult Parasite* (Encarsia formosa)

15   *Parasite eating red spider mite*

16   *Whitefly scales unparasitised and parasitised illustrating emergence hole of vacated parasitised scale*

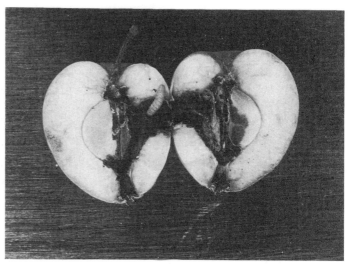

Codlin moth caterpillar tunnelling in apple

may then be removed in October and the pests destroyed. It is possible to purchase special bands for this purpose from horticultural sundriesmen.

TORTRIX MOTHS

There are a large number of tortrix moths whose caterpillars damage leaves and fruits. The rough and ready way of knowing which are tortrix caterpillars is to touch them on the head to see if they wriggle backwards quickly. This test isn't infallible but it usually works. DNC applied late February is effective for controlling this pest.

FRUIT-SURFACE EATING (*Caooe cia podana*)

The caterpillars are pale yellow and usually appear in July and August when they are about $\frac{1}{8}$ in. long. They generally get hold of a leaf and fasten it to an apple by means of a silken web. They then feed on the surface of the apple, often remaining on the fruits in this manner until they are gathered. Sometimes they just feed on the undersides of leaves and then, after the first moult, feed on the fruit. *Control Measures* Unfortunately, it is very difficult to control this pest. DNC washing should, of course, be carried out with force in February, and the use of a pyrethrum spray in July has proved effective.

Bud moth larva and two Tortrix moth larvae on apple
(Plant Protection)

BUD MOTH (*Spilonata ocellana*)
This form of tortrix known as the bud moth is a small, reddish-brown caterpillar with a black head. It enters the buds just before they start to grow in the spring and quickly ruins them. When the blossoms are opening, it migrates and feeds on the foliage, making for itself a little home with silken hairs in between several leaves. Sometimes it feeds on the fruits in August and September. *Control Measures* See Fruit-surface Eating Tortrix.

ERMINE MOTH (*Hyponomeuta malinella*)
Once this pest has been seen it is never forgotten. The small, spotted caterpillars live in conspicuous white nests of 'spider's web' like material which they build in the crutches of apple trees. They make their nests in May and continue to live in them till the end of June. The caterpillars defoliate the trees. *Control Measures* Spray the trees with a $7\frac{1}{2}$ per cent DNC wash

in January or February. Remove all nests of caterpillars seen in May and June.

Spray the trees with derris at the end of April and the beginning of May.

PITH MOTH (*Blastodacna atra*)

The caterpillar appears in May and June and attacks the shoots, burrowing inside them and inside the stems of flower trusses also. It is particularly bad in the case of young trees. As the result of the attack, the spur or shoot wilts and dies, and then the caterpillar may leave the twig and bore into another. It is brownish pink in colour, $\frac{1}{4}$ in. long when fully grown and has a dark brown head. *Control Measures* When regular spraying with a $7\frac{1}{2}$ per cent solution of a DNC wash is carried out the pith moth seldom appears. This spraying should be done during the month of January or February.

All infected shoots should be hand picked and burnt.

CASE BEARERS (*Eupista* spp and *Solenobia inconspicuella*)

The caterpillars of the case bearers live in a little shell or case, something like that of the snail, only it is cigar-like in shape. It feeds on the leaves, feeding first of all on the surface and then on the tissue inside. It produces irregular shaped bare patches by cutting out circular holes in the tissue.

There is another type of case bearer which has a pistol-shaped case, while the *Solenobia* has a greenish-grey case, three sided and straight. *Control Measures* Directly case bearers are seen damaging the leaves, spray with arsenate of lead, being sure to incorporate a spreader.

3   FLIES

SAWFLY (*Hoplocampa testudinea*)

One of the most serious pests of apples. It has been known for one hundred years. It must not be confused with the codling moth.

The sawfly lays its eggs just below the calyx of the flower. The caterpillar, which soon hatches out, bores into the side of the young fruit, leaving a sticky mess where it enters in. It often has more than one attempt at entering, forming a ribbon-like scar in this way.

The caterpillar is dirty white with a brown head and has a very objectionable odour. It may leave one fruit and enter

Apple sawfly damage (Plant Protection)

another. When matured late in June or early July it drops to
the ground and spends the winter as a cocoon in the soil.
Control Measures The tree should be sprayed with nicotine and
soft soap immediately after 80 per cent of the petals have fallen
(for formula, see chapter 13). The spray should be put on with
as much force as possible, and directed into the flower trusses,
where the insects will be laying their eggs.

Should this spraying have been omitted, and the caterpillars
be noticed later, then a good dusting with derris should be
given about sixteen days after petal-fall.

All infested fruits should be picked off and burnt should
either of the measures mentioned above not have been
adopted.

WASPS
Will not only attack plums and pears but will actually bite
pieces out of a ripe apple, either dessert or cooking.

The best method of controlling them is to find their nests
and to place a tablespoonful of fresh derris powder on a dry
day over the hole. The wasps when returning, send up a cloud
of dust by fanning their wings, and so take the derris into the
nest. All the grubs may not, however, be killed and so it is a
good plan to dig out the nest the following day. Where this is
impossible, a second or third application of derris dust near
the hole will be effective.

A handful of dust may be dropped into the entrance of each nest. If the nest is in the roof, it should be tackled at night time.

4   APHIDS, CAPSIDS, SCALES, etc.

APPLE CAPSID (*Plesiocoris rugicollis*)
The capsid bug is a comparatively new pest to apples. There are several different kinds, but the one mentioned here is the most important. It is found wherever fruit is grown in this country.

A small yellowish bug hatches out in April and May and may be seen running rapidly on the leaves and stems of apple trees on sunny days. It feeds on the under surface of leaves and on the tips of shoots. Little brown marks will be seen – as if puncture holes. These marks turn black later. If a leaf is removed and held up to the light the punctures show up clearly.

When the blossom has fallen the capsid starts to attack the fruits, puncturing the skin and causing rough corky patches to appear. The cork scars thus made can ruin fruits and make them look very unsightly.

When young, early in May, the bug is only $\frac{1}{18}$ in. long and yellowish green in colour. It moults five times, however, getting larger each time and gradually producing wings. When fully grown it is $\frac{1}{8}$ in. in length and green in colour.
Control Measures A DNC petroleum wash should be used and should be applied at a strength of $7\frac{1}{2}$ per cent in early March. A white oil petroleum wash is effective against capsid.

Spraying with nicotine and soft soap or a spreader (for formula, see chapter 13) should be done with as great a pressure as possible a week before the petals open.

A ring of grease-banding material should be placed around the trunks of the trees at the same time in order to prevent any bugs which fall to the ground from climbing up into the branches again.

APHIDS (*Aphis* spp.)
Eight different kinds of aphides or greenfly feed on apple trees, but the eggs of all of them may be killed by the DNC wash applied early in March. Such washes must be applied efficiently for if any part of the tree is missed, some aphis eggs will hatch out in the spring.

It is not proposed to describe the various aphides, some of

which are green, others of which are black, or of a plum colour.

A nicotine spray (for formula see chapter 13) should be applied in the spring directly the aphides are noticed if it is thought inadvisable to use the March wash.

WOOLLY APHIS (*Eriosoma lanigerum*)

The woolly aphis or American Blight is very well known. It attacks the trunks of trees and young wood, producing a white cotton-wool like substance which makes its attack very conspicuous. This wool-like substance may be present all the year round, but the pest is usually at its worst in the beginning of June till the end of October. It is important to keep it down because it may be the cause of transmitting the disease known as canker (see p. 120). *Control Measures* The trees should be fully covered with a white oil wash in March, applying the spray with as much force as possible and directing it into all the nooks and crannies – especially of old trees. A solution as advised by the manufacturers should be used.

In the spring, spraying should be done with nicotine and a spreader (formula 1 oz nicotine, 1 oz Shellestol, to 10 gallons of water). Those who do not wish to have the bother of making up such a wash may use a proprietary nicotine insecticide.

As nicotine is a poison, many prefer to use the non-poisonous liquid derris, which has given good results against this pest in Hertfordshire and Kent. In small gardens it is possible to hand paint with liquid derris, using it almost neat. This is far better than painting with methylated spirit.

APPLE SUCKER (*Psylla mali*)

In years gone by the apple sucker was a very serious pest, but since the advent of the tar distillate washes it has almost disappeared. The young suckers attack the opening flowers and quickly destroy them. This trouble is often erroneously described as frost damage. Trees that have refused to bear for fourteen years cropped the following year when sprayed by the author with a tar distillate wash in the winter! *Control Measures* Spray all trees as a routine measure with a DNC wash in February, using a 5 per cent solution. Be sure to cover the tree thoroughly.

Where the white oil wash has been omitted in February, spraying with derris and soft soap should be carried out just before the blossoms open.

MUSSEL SCALE (*Lepidosaphes ulmi*)
Little mussel-shell shaped scales will be found on the bark of trees. They are about $\frac{1}{8}$ in. in length, have a hard shell, being swollen and rounded at one end. They lie flat on the bark. *Control Measures* Spray the trees with a solution of a DNOC wash in February.

MITES and SPIDERS
The red spider or red mite which attacks apples and many other types of fruit trees are not controlled by tar distillate washes in the winter, though most of the insects that feed on them are! The result is that this pest has been increasing during the past few years.

Minute red bead-like eggs will be found on the under sides of spurs, in cracks in the trunk, and on the shoots. They are usually to be found in large masses and because they are bright red, can be seen from some distance away.

The mites hatch out towards the end of April or early in May and are yellowish or lightish red in colour. They feed on the under surface of the leaves, several broods developing in the summer. The leaves turn yellow or brown and assume the autumn tints long before the end of the summer. *Control Measures* Lime-sulphur gives an excellent control of red spider and so when trees are sprayed with this wash in order to control scab and mildew (see pp. 121–122) the spiders are kept down automatically.

Spray with a good liquid derris containing at least 0.004 per cent Rotenone in early June and repeat it in 2–3 weeks time. A Petroleum emulsion wash used in February kills the eggs very effectively.

HARES and RABBITS
Few people realise the damage that hares and rabbits can do in a night. They debark the trees – often ringing them completely, and they may even climb up into the crutch of bush trees, gnawing the branches for three feet above ground level. *Control Measures* See that the trees are wired round with narrow mesh wire or wire the whole orchard round carefully.

Heat tree banding grease until it runs freely, paint the stems of trees as far as rabbits and hares can reach with such material in September. Smear the trunks of the trees with Colophane. Plastic tree bands, like putters are ideal for young trees.

Cherry

1 CATERPILLARS

CHERRY FRUIT MOTH (*Argyresthia nitidella*)
This pest must not be confused with the Cherry Fruit Fly – an insect which damages the crop in France. The caterpillar of the moth is transparent green with a brown head. It enters the flower buds in the spring and by the time the blossoms open, it is feeding on the petals and stamens. Later it feeds on the young fruitlets. It can do a tremendous amount of damage and ruin the whole crop. *Control Measures* Spray with a 4 per cent white oil wash in late February. See that the trees are fully covered, using as much pressure as possible.

Most of the caterpillars which attack apples, attack cherries also. The control measures are similar in each case.

Spray with liquid derris or pyrethrum the moment the pest is seen.

2 FLIES

SAWFLIES
The two sawflies that attack cherries also attack pears. See **Pear.**

3 APHIDS, CAPSIDS AND SCALES

CHERRY BLACK-FLY (*Myzus cerasi*)
This black-fly infests the tips of branches, causing the leaves to curl and stunting the shoots. It is usually very conspicuous in May and June and then departs to another host in July. It is very difficult to get at the insects in the summer under the curled leaves, especially as the fruit is usually ripening at the time and it is obviously not desired to damage the crop. *Control Measures* Spray with a $7\frac{1}{2}$ per cent DNC solution in early March and thus kill the eggs. To get good results it is necessary to have a perfect covering.

Where, for some reason or another, DNC washing was omitted, the trees should be sprayed about the middle of April with nicotine and Shellestol.

Formula: $\frac{3}{4}$ oz nicotine, 1 oz of a detergent to 10 gal. water.

Cherries may also be attacked by capsids (see **Currants**) and by mussel scale (for control, see **Apple**).

Currants, Black, Red and White

1   CATERPILLARS

CURRANT CLEARWING (*Conopia tipuliformis*)
Mainly attacks the blackcurrant but also damages the red-currants and gooseberries. The caterpillar bores in the stems, the leaves wilt on the shoot and the fruit trusses do not mature. It is fully grown by April and is then white in colour with a brown head. *Control Measures* Go over the bushes in the winter, bending over the end growths or tips. Those that are weak because of the tunnelling will snap off. When this happens the remainder of the shoot should be cut back to sound wood and the infected material burnt.

SHOOT-BORER (*Lampronia capitella*)
The caterpillars bore into the stems and buds in the spring. The leaves wilt and the shoot eventually dies. Later it may attack the fruits, the baby caterpillar being found inside feeding on the seed. The caterpillars are bright red first of all but turn greenish white as they reach maturity. *Control Measures* Infested shoots should be removed in April when they are seen. The bushes should be sprayed with a 4 per cent solution of a white oil wash in late February, the wash being put on with considerable force, so as to get at the cocoons which are hiding in cracks and under the rind.

2   FLIES

GOOSEBERRY SAWFLY
A small caterpillar which eats the leaves and may defoliate the bush. (For control see **Gooseberry**.)

3   APHIDS, CAPSIDS and MITES

CAPSID BUG (*Lygus pabulinus*)
This capsid is very similar in appearance to the apple capsid bug.
   It may attack gooseberries, blackberries, cherries, rasp-berries, strawberries, pears and peaches, as well as currants. It hatches out in April, attacking the young leaves and causing minute brown spots and holes to form in them. When the terminal bud is attacked, large numbers of side shoots develop.

In the case of gooseberries the fruit will be badly marked by brownish-yellowish patches and the skin may crack. In the case of pears, brownish-black spots appear on the leaves, and on the fruits irregular pitted, corky tissues will develop. On plums the foliage will be spotted and pitted. On strawberries similar damage is done; on blackberries the damage is often severe and the holes that develop after attack are very often large and conspicuous.

The eggs are laid just under the bark of one or two-year old shoots. The bugs hatch out in April and feed on the young foliage. Like the apple capsids they moult several times, and during part of their life may feed on weeds and other plants. When fully grown they fly about readily. On first hatching out the bug is semi-transparent, small and shiny, and of a pale yellowish-green colour, but fully grown it is of a bright green colour. *Control Measures* A spraying should be given with a DNC petroleum wash at $7\frac{1}{2}$ per cent early in March.

Spraying may also be done with nicotine late in April, and again about mid May. (For formula see chapter 13).

When the bugs feel a jar on the tree, caused by the spray or the operator, they drop to the ground where they live on weeds if the land is not kept clean or is not mown regularly as a lawn. Some consider it worthwhile, therefore, to spray the ground as well as the trees.

3   APHIDS

APHIDS

Various types of aphids or greenfly attack currants, sucking the underneath of the leaves and causing the foliage to curl up and turn red in colour. The new wood growth may be deformed and the fruit may be covered with the secretion of the aphids and not develop to its proper size. *Control Measures* Spray with a $7\frac{1}{2}$ per cent DNC wash in early March. Soak the bushes thoroughly. Where this has been omitted for some reason or another, spray in the spring with nicotine and soft soap (for formula, see chapter 13) before the leaves begin to curl. Usually towards the end of April. Spraying is useless once the leaves have curled, and then the only thing to do is to mix up a nicotine and soft soap wash and go round the bushes, dipping the tips of the leaf curled shoots into the solution.

4 BIG BUD

BIG BUD (*Eriophyes ribis*)
The big bud mite or blackcurrant gall mite does more damage to blackcurrant bushes than any other pest known. In blackcurrants the big buds produced make the attack very obvious. When, however, the mite attacks red, white currants, or gooseberries, the buds merely die and go brown.

The mite itself is microscopical, being only $\frac{1}{100}$ in. in length. It is not visible to the naked eye, being white and semi-transparent. It lives on the leaves from March to the end of June, and in June or early July works its way into the bud of the new year's growth where it lays its eggs. There may easily be, at the end of the winter, 10,000 mites and more in one bud. In the spring, usually the end of March, and early in April, when the new leaves are unfolding, they escape from the buds in order to move on to new homes. *Control Measures* The bushes should be sprayed with lime-sulphur about the end of March or the first week of April, just after the flower racemes appear but before the blossom opens. This is usually when the leaves are about the size of a 10p piece. The formula is 1 pt lime-sulphur to 20 pts water, except in the case of *Goliath, Davison's 8* and *Wellington XXX*, when the concentration should be 1 pt lime-sulphur to 50 pts water, because these varieties may be damaged by the stronger solution.

The big bud mite is considered to be the carrier of the virus disease, Reversion, and it is, therefore, most important to prevent mite attacks from spreading. Lime-sulphur spraying should, therefore, be done every year as an insurance.

Other pests that may attack currants are Weevils, Winter Moths, Mottled Umber Caterpillar, Mussel Scale and Red Spider (see **Apple**).

Gooseberry

GOOSEBERRY SAWFLY (*Nematus* spp and *Pristiphora pallipes*)
There are various sawfly caterpillars which attack gooseberries; some are green, spotted with black dots, some are pale green and have a black head, while others are dark green with a lighter coloured head. The caterpillars feed very rapidly and bushes can often be completely denuded of foliage before the gardener is aware of their presence.

They first appear in April and May, there is usually a

Magpie or currant moth larvae

second generation in June, and a third about mid August. With the *Pristiphora* there are four broods in a season. *Control Measures* As the sawflies lay their eggs on the leaves in the centre of the bushes near the ground, quite good control may be achieved by spraying the centre of the bushes at the end of April with a pyrethrum spray. Dust or spray with derris as soon as sawfly damage is noticed, before the little caterpillars have worked their way all over the bushes and so become almost inaccessible to control.

Where the pests have been overlooked until the fruit is almost ready for picking, spraying with liquid derris should be done instead.

APHIDS (*Aphis grossulariae* and *Eriosoma ulmi*)

There are two kinds of aphids or greenfly found on gooseberries; the one attacks the shoots and the other the roots.

The aphis attacking the shoots is dark green and plump. It feeds on the tips in the spring, crumpling the leaves and deforming the shoots. The whole bush may be stunted thereby. Ants love this particular species and are always in attendance. They usually are the first to indicate the presence of the trouble.

The aphids that attack the roots (also attacking the roots of red and blackcurrants) produce a white woolly-like substance below ground level, and check the bushes severely. It is seldom that the damage is realised till the bushes are dug out. *Control Measures* Spray with DNC, using a $7\frac{1}{2}$ per cent solution in February. Spray the bushes in May with derris wash so as to give the shoots a thorough soaking.

In the case of the root form, dip the roots of young trees in nicotine and soft soap (for formula, see chapter 13) before planting them in their permanent positions.

RED SPIDER (*Bryobia praetiosa*)

A very serious disease of gooseberries. Can cause a tremendous amount of damage in a week or two. The leaves go pale yellow and look as if they have been fired. Usually they drop off. The whole plant will look sickly, the fruit being undersized.

The mites, which are usually greenish, greyish or rusty red, will be found underneath the leaves, sucking the sap. They feed only on warm sunny days. On cold days they retire to the lower leaves and rest. They usually leave the gooseberry bushes in June and do not return again till the following spring. *Control Measures* Spray the bushes with a 4 per cent solution of DNC wash in February. As the mites usually migrate to the bushes, however, in the spring, this is not always successful.

Spray with a 2 per cent lime-sulphur solution directly after the flowering period, taking care to wet the under surfaces of the leaves, and giving the centre of the bushes special treatment.

With varieties that are sulphur-shy, like *Leveller, Gunner* and *Keen's Seedling,* spray with a 2 per cent solution of a white oil emulsion instead.

Other pests which may attack gooseberries are Currant Clearwing (see **Currants**), Winter Moth Caterpillars (see **Apple**), Capsids (see **Apple** and **Currants**), Mussel Scale (see **Apple**), and Gall Mites (see Big Bud in **Black currants**).

Loganberry, blackberry, phenomenal berry, etc

RASPBERRY BEETLE (*Byturus tomontosus*)
The raspberry beetle is often wrongly called the Raspberry Weevil. It is perhaps a more serious pest of loganberries than of raspberries and blackberries. The beetle appears in May and may be seen on the canes when the flower buds open. It is brownish-yellow at first, turning to greyish-brown, and about $\frac{1}{6}$ in. in length. It lays its eggs in the blossoms during June or July, white grubs hatch out and these feed on the forming fruits and tunnel into the 'plugs'. *Control Measures* Spray with liquid derris ten days after flowering begins, to destroy the beetles. Give a second application, if necessary, ten days later. The first spraying usually has to be done about the middle of June and the second spraying about the end of June. With blackberries, the application should be made the first week of July and again the third week of July.

A fine spray should be used and all parts of the flowers and fruits should be wetted. Derris may be used, if necessary, instead of liquid sprays but these are never as effective.

BLACKBERRY MITE (*Eriophyes essigi*)
Minute microscopic mites attack the fruits, malforming them, and causing uneven ripening. The berries often have an abnormal red appearance which has caused American workers to call this trouble the Red-Berry Disease.

The tranlucent mites hibernate until the end of February under the bud scales or in the dried-up fruits. By flowering time they have bred and migrate to the blossoms. *Control Measures* Spray with lime-sulphur when the new growths are about 5 in. long.
Formula: 1 pt lime-sulphur to 12 pts water. Repeat the spray when the new growths are 9 in. long.

Remove and burn off old canes as soon as possible after fruiting.

BRAMBLE-SHOOT WEBBER (*Notocelia uddmanniana*)
This is one of the tortrix caterpillars, dusky browny-red in

colour with a black head, though the newly hatched caterpillar is whitish.

It feeds on the leaves in May and June, particularly at the tips, and may nibble the terminal growth, thus causing laterals to develop. It usually draws the leaves together and feeds in the centre of the young growths. Eventually the terminal bud is completely destroyed and the surrounding leaves webbed together. *Control Measures* Cut off the webbed leaves, as these contain the caterpillars, and burn them. Do this in May.

Spray in April with liquid derris, giving a drench.

Other pests that attack these cane fruits are Capsids (see **Currants**) and Aphides (see **Raspberry**).

Peach, nectarine and apricot

APHIDES (*Myzus persicae, Anuraphis schwartzi*) etc.
A large number of species of aphides or greenfly attack apricots, nectarines and peaches. The two principal ones, however, are the Almond Aphis and Peach Aphis. The latter is greenish yellow or brownish pink, and feeds on the young leaves, causing conspicuous leaf-curl.

Sometimes the blossoms will be infested and deformed. The former is yellowish green, amber, yellow or reddish, though some colonies may be black. The aphides attack the leaves, curling the foliage, and in bad cases the trees will be left almost bare because of leaf fall. *Control Measures* Spray the trees with a 5 per cent solution of a DNOC wash in February. Do not delay till later or there will be a danger of the wash injuring the buds. Other pests which may attack apricots, nectarines and peaches are Winter Moth Caterpillars (see **Apple**), Tortrix Caterpillars (see **Apple**), Wasps (see **Apple**), Mussel Scale (see **Apple**), Red Spider (see **Apple**), and Capsids (see **Currants**), Mealy Aphids (see **Plum**).

Pear

SLUG WORMS (*Caliroa limacina*)
This pest feeds on the foliage of both pears and cherries and sometimes attacks apples and plums. The caterpillar looks like a dark green or blackish slug and feeds entirely on the upper surface of the leaves, making them patchy and blotchy. The trouble is usually at its worst from the middle of June until leaf-fall. *Control Measures* Spray with liquid derris the moment

slug worms are seen, or spray with nicotine. Dust may be used instead of sprays. Be sure to apply the wash directly the slug worms are first seen.

PEAR SAWFLY (*Social Sawfly*) (*Neurotoma flaviventris*)

The true pear sawfly is very rare. The social pear sawfly is sometimes quite common. It may feed on plums and cherries as well as pears. The caterpillars are orange yellow and have pale brown stripes down each side of their bodies. Their heads are black and shiny. They live in white tents which they make on the leaves and shoots, varying from 3 in. to 12 in. in length. These are usually to be found from the beginning of July till the end of August. The caterpillars are very clumsy when they move and they wriggle violently when disturbed. When frightened they exude a clear blood-red fluid from behind their head. *Control Measures* Remove the tents in July immediately they are seen, thus destroying the caterpillars.

PEAR MIDGE (*Contarinia pyrivora*)

One of the most important pests of pears. Seems more partial to *Fertility* and *Williams* while *Conference* often escapes. The maggots infest the young fruits which grow rapidly as compared with the others. They soon, however, become deformed and when they are cut open, a black cavity will be found inside filled with little white maggots. The damage is usually noticed from the middle of May to the second week of June. *Control Measures* Spray the ground around the infected trees with a tar oil or with dinitro-orthocresol petroleum oil wash, using at least $\frac{1}{4}$ gal diluted wash per sq. yd. Do not spray the trees themselves, or the foliage will be injured, for this spraying must be done between the bud burst and white bud stages. Don't spray with very high pressure so that the spray does not drift on to the trees.

Cultivate the ground thoroughly from the second week of June till the second week of July; regular hoeings have to be done each week. This method destroys the maggot as it goes to hibernate for the winter.

APHIDS

The aphids or greenfly which attack pears are not at all important. It is seldom that they give much trouble. *Control Measures* See **Apple.**

PEAR LEAF BLISTER MOTH (*Eriophyes piri*)
This mite is microscopical like the big bud mite. It attacks the upper surface of leaves thus causing them to become dotted with greenish-yellow or yellowish-red blisters. The old blisters turn brown and finally black. Fruits may be attacked too, reddish or brown pustules of irregular shape being formed. *Control Measures* The trees should be sprayed with a 5 per cent solution of a lime-sulphur wash during the first or second week of March. All the buds should be wetted thoroughly since at that time the mites will be found there.

Other pests that may be found on pears include Leopard Moth Caterpillar (see **Apple**), Vapourer Moth Caterpillar (see **Apple**), Codling Moth Caterpillar (see **Apple**), Tortrix Moth Caterpillar (see **Apple**), Wasps (see **Apple**), Twig Cutters (see **Apple**), Shot-hole Borers (see **Plum**).

Plum and damson

SHOT-HOLE BORER BEETLE (*Anisandrus dispar*)
These tiny black beetles attack plum, damson, apple, pear, cherry and other fruit trees. They are particularly bad where plums are attacked by bacterial canker. There are various species, all of which tunnel into the bark and trunks of fruit trees. There they bore galleries and lay eggs, two broods often appearing in a year.

Trees that are attracted by these little beetles usually have a most peculiar smell. *Control Measures* Remove dead and dying branches that are attacked by these boring beetles. In bad cases it may be necessary to remove whole trees and burn them.

Where only the lower portion of a tree is attacked, spray this in April with a Pysect aerosol, directing the spray into the holes. Care should be taken not to allow the young shoots or foliage to be touched with the spray at this time of the year.

Paint the trunks of attacked trees with a paraffin wax in March or April with the object of stopping up the holes. Spray with a 10 per cent DNC wash in March, try and keep the spray off the green buds.

RED PLUM MAGGOT (*Cydia junebrana*)
This maggot which infests plums, damsons and peaches, is unfortunately very common. The caterpillar is bright red, and feeds on the fruits from the middle of June onwards. It makes a

hole near the base and bores into the fruit, the caterpillar tunnelling into the flesh near the stone.

When fully grown at the end of August or early in September it comes out of the fruit and hides under the bark or in cracks and crevices where it spins a cocoon. *Control Measures* Spray with a strong derris wash in September. Give a good drenching so as to make certain to get into the cracks and crevices.

Spray in the summer with liquid derris, about the middle of June, just at the time when the caterpillars are hatching. This kills the maggots before they enter the fruits.

PLUM SAWFLY (*Hoplocampa flara*)
A very common pest. Its favourite varieties are *Victoria*, *Czar* and *Belle de Louvaine*. *Pond's Seedling* and *Monarch* seem to be resistant.

The eggs are laid in the flowers and the little caterpillars that hatch out enter the fruits. The trouble can usually be detected by the sticky substance and black frass that exude from the hole. When fully grown the caterpillar is $\frac{1}{2}$ in. long, and has a creamy white body and yellowish-brown head. It has ten pairs of legs. *Control Measures* Spray the tree with liquid derris giving a good drench just after the blossoms have fallen. Spray again a week later.

If it is necessary to dust, dusting should not be done until fourteen days after petal-fall, using derris dust.

APHIDS (*Anuraphis padi* and *Hyalopterus arundinis*)
Anuraphis is the leaf-curling kind and *Hyalopterus* the mealy aphis. Neither of them is very important these days since the advent of the winter wash.

In neglected orchards or where trees are never sprayed with tar oil in the winter, these two aphides do a tremendous amount of harm, for they not only damage the leaves by sucking them, but they reduce the vigour of the trees so much that they fail to crop the following season also. In many districts damsons never crop year after year, entirely owing to aphis attacks. *Control Measures* Spray with DNC wash in early March. It is important to spray as early as this for the buds of some plum varieties like *Belle de Louvain* and the *Myrobolan plum* are damaged if the spray is applied much later.

Those that miss spraying plums in March should spray in the spring with nicotine and soft soap (for formula, see chapter

13) before leaf-curling takes place. In the case of the mealy plum aphis, a miscible white oil should be used instead of the nicotine spray for these aphids have a waxy covering.

BULLFINCHES
Bullfinches can cause serious damage to growth and crop by eating the buds during the dormant season. In serious cases all the flower and many of the wood buds are destroyed. As a result there is little or no crop. *Control Measures* Stretch black cotton in and among the branches. Be liberal with the cotton and you will frighten the Bullfinches away. Spraying in February with a deterrent called Cunitex has been successful.

NATURAL ENEMIES
Plum aphids are eaten by many predators including ladybirds and their grubs, the grubs of lacewings and hover flies and anthocorid bugs. They are also attacked by the grubs of minute wasps. These natural enemies become very numerous when the aphid attack is at its full height. Do not think that they definitely do no good, because by killing off vast numbers of aphids, they prevent even more severe attacks the following year.

MITES AND SPIDERS
On plums and damsons it is quite a good plan to spray the trees with a summer white-oil and derris using a 2 per cent solution ten days after petal-fall. A second spraying may be necessary in bad cases ten days later.

Other pests that may attack plums and damsons are Leopard Moth (see **Apple**), Lackey Moth (see **Apple**), Winter Moth Caterpillar (see **Apple**), Tortrix Caterpillar (see **Apple**), Wasps (see **Apple**), Red Spider (see **Apple**), Red-legged Weevil (see **Raspberry**), Capsid (see **Currants**).

Raspberry

RED-LEGGED WEEVIL (*Otiorrhynchus clavipes*)
This weevil attacks the blossoms, minute fruitlets and un-opened buds. It may gnaw at shoots and cause them to break. It may feed on the foliage, making little round holes in the leaves. It may bore into the young canes near the base and check the growth. The weevil mainly feeds at night and is diffi-cult to find during the day as it hides under stones, rubbish, clods of earth, etc.

The weevil is black and has red legs. It appears late in April and early in May. *Control Measures* It is very difficult to control, but it is worthwhile tapping the canes at night time, holding out boards covered with banding grease. This work has to be done without the aid of a light because these pests fall to the ground directly they see any light or hear movement.

Another method is to make up a bait consisting of 1 lb. apple pulp, 1 lb. bran or wheat chaff, $\frac{1}{10}$ lb. sodium fluosilicate. These three should be mixed together and sprinkled along the rows. The mixture acts as a poison bait.

CLAY-COLOURED WEEVIL (*Otiorrhynchus singularis*)
This clay-coloured weevil does similar damage to the red-legged weevil, but it usually starts its attack at the end of March and early in April, when it feeds on the leaf stalks, causing them to wilt. *Control Measures* See Red-Legged Weevil above.

RASPBERRY-MOTH (*Lampronia rubiella*)
A very important pest. The canes when attacked will be found at the end of April or early in May to have withered shoots on them, the insides of which are tunnelled. The grub that does this feeds on the pith, and is red in colour, though the chrysalis that it forms later is brown. It must not be confused with the grub of the Bramble-shoot Webber (see **Loganberry**).

In addition to the damage it does in April to the cane, the grub feeds on the plug of the fruit about June, though its damage is often unnoticed. It hibernates at the base of the canes in the rubbish or on the stakes at the ends of the rows. *Control Measures* The canes should be sprayed with an 8 per cent solution of a white oil wash in January. This will destroy the hibernating grubs and as a matter of fact, any aphis eggs there may be on the canes as well.

APHIDES
There are several species of aphides which attack raspberries, some of them curl the leaves and some of them just suck the sap. None of them does a great deal of damage. *Control Measures* Should it be necessary to control the aphides, spray the canes in the winter with a 5 per cent solution of a DNC wash. The eggs will thus be smothered.

Other pests that may attack raspberries are Raspberry Beetle (see **Loganberry**), Vapourer Moth Caterpillar (see

Apple), Tortrix Moth Caterpillar (see **Apple**), Bud Moth Maggot (see **Apple**).

Strawberry

GROUND BEETLES
There are six different kinds of beetles which attack strawberries, four of which damage the ripening fruits. They usually do more damage on warm nights. *Control Measures* It is not easy to check these beetles. Dressings of naphthalene at 2 oz to the sq. yd seem to drive them away without doing harm to the plants.

It is most important to keep the rows hoed regularly in order to move the hiding places and expose the pests. The mulching of the rows with dark brown powdery compost or medium grade sedge peat prevents any trouble from these beetles.

STRAWBERRY BLOSSOM WEEVIL (*Anthonomus rubi*)
This is strawberry circles, is often known as the Elephant Beetle. It lives not only on the strawberry but on the raspberry and blackberry as well. The variety Royal Sovereign is particularly susceptible to attack.

The weevil itself is black. It appears in April and May and lays its eggs in the unopened flowers. It makes a puncture hole with its long snout in order to do this. It then either partially or completely cuts through the stalk of the bud and prevent it developing further. Most of the damage is seen in June. *Control Measures* Apply a derris dust as soon as the first trace of the trouble is noticed. Give a second application a week or ten days later.

STRAWBERRY MOTH (*Peronea conariana*)
This is sometimes called the Leaf Button Moth. The caterpillar appears in late April or early May and feeds on the unopened leaves and on the blossom buds as they develop. It often joins several leaves together by means of silken threads and it may make a web on the under side of the foliage inside which it may feed. When disturbed it is active and wriggles about freely. It is greenish – the back being darker than the head, which is shiny yellow. It is fully grown by September. *Control Measures* In May or early June spray with liquid derris for it is dangerous as late as this to spray with arsenate.

In very bad cases the tops of the plants should be cut off in

September down to the crown, the tops being removed and burnt.

APHIDS

There are many species of aphides or green fly that attack strawberries, perhaps the most important of which has the Latin name of *Capitophorus fragaefolii*. This is the aphis which carries virus disease from diseased to healthy plants, any time between March and September. It is lighter in colour than the normal greenfly, being almost yellow. It lives on the strawberry plants from the latter part of August till the following July and doesn't seem to be worried by frost, snow or cold winds. *Control Measures* As aphids are the carriers of the virus diseases, it is most important to try and control them. The only method which we have found really satisfactory is to spray with nicotine and soft soap: 1 oz nicotine, 1 lb. soft soap, and 10 gal. water. The plants should be given a thorough soaking in April, and again in May. Liquid seaweed using it as a spray or liquid manure is a strong deterrent to aphis and red spider as well as being a good nutrient.

Immediately after picking the straw, which has been put down to keep the fruit clean alongside the rows, should be set alight. In this way large numbers of the leaves are burnt off and the aphids thus destroyed. In addition, red spiders and other pests will be killed. The plants will scarcely be harmed thereby and many growers affirm that they are much stronger the following year as the result.

TARSONEMID MITE (*Tarsonemus pallidus*)

This mite occurs all over the country. It is very troublesome, not only because it injures the plant directly, but also because it so disfigures that leaves that it makes it difficult to be certain whether a plant is attacked by the Yellow Edge virus or not.

It feeds in the folds of small, unexpanded leaves, from the middle of May until well on in November. As a result, the older leaves become puckered and crinkled, the young leaves may be killed, and the plant loses its fresh green colour. In bad cases, multiple crowns are formed and runners are killed. It is not known how the mites pass from plant to plant or from garden to garden. *Control Measures* Spray with a 3 per cent solution of lime-sulphur, plus a spreader, during the third week of March, giving the plants a thorough soaking. Repeat a spraying with lime-sulphur after picking is over and apply a seaweed fertiliser at 3 oz to the sq. yd.

Immerse all strawberries before planting in water, kept at a temperature of exactly 110° F. for 20 mins. This kills all the mites present, and other pests too, of course. Cool the plants off immediately after this treatment, by plunging them into cold water. Plant immediately afterwards.

This warm-water treatment is the *only* satisfactory way of controlling the Tarsonemid Mite.

STRAWBERRY RHYNCHITES (*Rhynchites germanicus and R. R. minutus*)
This is a stem-cutting weevil which not only cuts the stems of the leaves but of the fruits also, and may work systematically over the plants, crippling them. The damage is notable in May and continues right through the month of June. The stems are often cut halfway through only, but even in this case the leaves will flag and die. *Control Measures* Dust with a derris dust directly the first sign of damage is noticed. Repeat the dusting a week or ten days later if the infestation persists.

Sometimes this pest will spread to the blackberry and loganberry.

Other pests that attack strawberries are Chafer beetles (see chapter 3), Wireworms (see chapter 3), Leather Jackets (see chapter 3), Slugs (see chapter 3), Eelworms (see chapter 3 and chapter 12) and Red Spider (see above).

10   The diseases of fruit

ARMILLARIA ROOT ROT (*Armillaria mellea*)
This disease, sometimes called the Honey Fungus, and
sometimes the Bootlace Fungus, is really one of the common
toadstools. It lives on the roots of trees, producing black
strands which look like black string, hence the name bootlace.
Trees attacked soon die, and then the toadstools are seen
above ground. Their stalks are often seven or eight inches long,
yellow brown and dark brown at the base. The cap is honey
coloured above and bears brown scales, the toadstools are
usually in dense clusters. They are found from July to
December, but are most prolific about October. *Control
Measures* Every diseased tree must be removed as soon as possible. When woodlands are being planted up with fruit trees,
care must be taken to remove all the roots and stumps, even
gate posts and fencing poles may be attacked. Experiments in
America seem to show that the disease can be killed with
carbon bi-sulphide which should be injected into the ground
to a depth of 8 or 9 in. There are injectors specially made for
the purpose. This chemical should be injected every 2 ft all
over the infected ground and thirty to sixty days are required
before the fungus is completely killed. Another method is to
make holes 9 or 10 in. deep every 2 ft around the tree and 4 ft
away from the main trunk. Into the bottom of each hole should
be dropped a teaspoonful of carbon bisulphide. The hole
should then be filled in.

APPLE CANKER (*Nectria galligena*)
A most serious disease which, if neglected, will cause the death
of the tree. It can be recognised in the early stages by a sunken
area of bark round a bud or open wound. These areas tend to
spread lengthwise along the branch or stem in raised rings,
making them look rather like oyster shells.

The tissues around the canker increase and the branch
becomes swollen and distorted. The bark is killed and the
dead portions discoloured.

The spores of the fungus enter the tree through wounds left

120

when pruning or by cracks due to Scab, or even through the leaf scars when the leaves fall in the autumn.

Some varieties are more susceptible than others, these being *Cox's Orange Pippin, Lord Suffield, Warner's King, James Grieve,* and *Worcester Pearmain. Bramley's Seedling, Lane's Prince Albert* and *Newton Wonder* are most resistant.

Root stock also has an influence on the degree of resistance of a variety, *Worcester Pearmain* being most resistant on root stocks nos. 1 and 5 and far less resistant on nos. 4 and 7. The new *Malling-Merton* stocks are all often resistant.

In areas that have been infected for a long time the centres become ridged and cracks appear. In these cracks bright red egg-like bodies can be seen – only just visible to the naked eye (but easily seen with a hand lens). By these the disease is increased, the rain washing them on to the other parts of the tree, and even the fruit is attacked and becomes another source of infection. *Control Measures* If trees are very badly attacked dig them up and burn them. If a branch is badly attacked, cut back well below the canker. If the canker is on the surface, remove all infected bark and wood. All cut surfaces must be painted with a thick coating of white lead paint. All mummified fruits must be burnt.

Routine spraying with Bordeaux mixture helps to control the disease as it reduces Scab infections on the young twigs and, therefore, less infection via Scab wounds. It must be done twice at leaf fall and again at bud burst.

Painting the wound (after cutting out the diseased parts) with Medo does good.

Woolly Aphis must also be kept in control (see **Apple,** chapter 9), as the disease enters through the injuries caused by this pest and through the leaf scars after abscission.

Low-lying, badly drained soil with a heavy sub-soil is conducive to canker and care should be taken not to plant susceptible varieties on such a site. Avoid heavy dressings of nitrogenous manure.

APPLE MILDEW (*Podosphoera leucotricha*)

A common disease attacking young shoots and foliage or flower buds. This fungus can live through the winter in buds which have become infected the previous season, and shows itself when the tree first comes into leaf. Those leaves that are attacked are narrow and curled, and covered with mealy powder – the shoots becoming distorted and stunted in growth. The flower buds attacked produce smaller and paler flowers than usual and these do not set fruit.

The spores from this first attack are blown by the wind and further infection occurs on shoots and leaves and fruit, though the latter is not seriously attacked as a rule.

The most susceptible varieties are *Lane's Prince Albert, Cox's Orange Pippin, Bismarck, Bramley's Seedling. Worcester Pearmain* is one of the more resistant varieties. *Control Measures* Spraying and pruning out infected shoots are the two main methods of control. In winter infected shoots are pale grey in colour and should be cut out before the spring. In the spring when the leaves come out, it is possible to cut out those shoots showing mildew.

Mildew may be controlled by application of sulphur in powder form – either flowers of sulphur, a ground sulphur, or in the form of liquid lime-sulphur, or even colloidal sulphur.

Some varieties such as *Stirling Castle* and *Lane's Prince Albert* are 'sulphur-shy' and for these varieties the pruning out of infected shoots should be done as thoroughly as possible, or a soad and soap spray may be used.

BLOSSOM WILT (*Sclerotinia laxa*)

A common disease in the south of England and often occurring in other parts. Chiefly attacks the flowers. Recognised by the wilting of the blossom trusses about a fortnight after they have come into flower. The spurs are killed with their flowers and leaves and sometimes the fungus extends into the branch for a foot or so, following a canker.

Very susceptible varieties are *Lord Derby, Cox's Orange Pippin, James Grieve, Rival* and *Ecklinville Seedling.* Many others are also attacked. *Bramley's Seedlings* are rarely attacked by blossom wilt. *Control Measures* Winter and summer pruning out of all infected spurs and cankerous wood. Wilting spurs should be removed at once so that the fungus has no chance to spread into the branch. Spraying with lime-sulphur in the spring helps to control this disease.

APPLE SCAB (*Venturia inaequalis*)

The most troublesome of all apple diseases. It attacks young shoots making wounds by which canker spores can enter; infects the foliage and, most serious of all, the fruit, making it unsightly and unsaleable when severely attacked. If attacked in the early stages the fruit becomes misshapen and cracked and may often fall early. If infected later they develop normally with large spots on the skin.

The disease is first seen as dark spots; later the spots become greenish and corky. The spots developing when the apples are in store are nearly round in shape, and are sunken and pitch black. *Cox's Orange Pippin, Worcester Pearmain* and *Laxton's Superb* are some of the most susceptible varieties.

King Edward VII is one of the most resistant varieties. *Bramley's Seedling*, thought to be resistant, is now considered doubtful, as some serious attacks on this variety have been recorded recently. *Control Measures* It is necessary to cut out all shoots with scab wounds on them as it is in these scabs that the spores are produced and cause new infection in spring. The prunings must be burnt and, if feasible, any old leaves from the infected trees.

It is essential to carry out a spraying programme if this disease is to be satisfactorily controlled. Two applications at least should be given, but four are advisable. Where only two are given these should be B and C.

(A) In the 'green bud' stage – when the flower bud is still enclosed by a rosette of leaves.

(B) In the 'pink bud' stage – when the petals are clearly showing, but the flower is quite short.

(C) In the petal-fall stage – directly the petals have fallen.

(D) Two or three weeks after.

If pre-blossom spraying were not thorough, or if the season is wet and specially conducive to scab infection, later sprayings may be necessary to control a late infection, storage scab, and infection of leaves and twigs where the fungus lives during the winter.

Usually the infection is not bad in small gardens and in this case it is only necessary to spray in the pink bud and post-blossom stages. The washes used are Bordeaux mixture, lime-sulphur, colloidal sulphur and colloidal copper. The colloidal mixtures are recommended for late spraying only as they are more expensive but not most effective, but they do not leave a deposit on the fruit.

Bordeaux mixture is generally safe to use on *Bramley's Seedling, Newton Wonder, Allington Pippin* and *Worcester Pearmain,* but not on *Cox's Orange Pippin. Beauty of Bath* and *Lord Derby* are also particularly susceptible to copper sprays, so a weak solution of lime-sulphur should be used.

Other varieties such as *Lane's Prince Albert* and *Stirling Castle* are what is known as 'sulphur-shy' and suffer from leaf scorch and defoliation if sprayed with sulphur sprays.

Choice of spray is influenced by the variety of the apple and also if the control of red spider is to be considerd – if so, lime-sulphur will help in this case, but not the copper preparation.

The following spray programme is to be recommended:

(1) Green Bud. Lime-sulphur spray $2\frac{1}{2}$ per cent in strength except 1 per cent for *Lane's Prince Albert* and not to be used at all for *Stirling Castle*.

(2) Pink Bud. Lime-sulphur as for Green Bud stage. Lead arsenate at the rate of 1 lb. lead arsenate paste or $\frac{1}{4}$ lb. powder to 25 gal. water may be added to the spray in both cases if attack by caterpillar is severe. Nicotine at the rate of 2 fl. oz per 25 gal. wash may be added to Pink Bud spray to control Capsid Bug.

(3) Petal Fall. Lime-sulphur 1 per cent and Nicotine at 2 fl. oz per 25 gal.

Beauty of Bath, Duchess, Favourite, Lane's Prince Albert and *Stirling Castle* should be omitted from this application as they are sulphur-shy and also fairly Scab-resistant.

Charles Ross, Grenadier, Early Victoria, King Edward VII, Lord Derby, Mr Gladstone, are also generally resistant to Scab and should only be sprayed at this stage to control Red Spider. The Scab repetitive cycle can be broken by encouraging complete rotting of last year's leaves. So water these well 'in situ' with Farmura when diluted.

(4) Two or three weeks after, repeat as for petal-fall stage, omitting nicotine unless aphis is present, then use at the rate of 1 oz per 20 gal.

As mentioned, in small gardens it is usually only necessary to spray at the pink bud and after petal-fall stages.

SOOTY BLOTCH (*Gloeodes pomigena*)

This disease attacks the growing fruit and continues to develop during storage. The fruit attacked looks as if someone with sooty fingers had handled it, leaving smoky, smudgy marks. The marks are about $\frac{1}{4}$ in. in size, spreading into each other, they sometimes cover a large portion of the fruit with brownish-green blotches.

This disease is affected by the weather and is most prevalent in cold wet summers, and the infection is heaviest on the shadiest parts of the tree and on branches in the middle or on the north side of the tree.

Most varieties are susceptible to Sooty Blotch, especially *Bramley's Seedling,* and sometimes *Cox's Orange Pippin* is badly attacked. *Control Measures* Careful pruning of the trees to prevent overgrowing of branches and to let in light and air. Ordinary spray programme with Bordeaux or lime-sulphur will help to check the disease. If, however, the control is not sufficient, it is necessary to treat the infected fruit before it is stored. This is done by mixing $\frac{1}{2}$ lb. chloride of lime (bleaching powder) in 1 gal. water, stirring well. Next morning pour off the clear liquid, immerse the fruit in this liquid for one minute, expose to the air for ten minutes, then wash under tap water and leave in the air to dry. For large quantities the fruit should be put in a tray and left there throughout the process until the fruit is dry.

BROWN ROT (*Sclerotinia fructigena*)
This disease attacks fruit soon after it has set till it is ripe, and may even continue to develop in the store.

It is recognised by rings of yellowish cushion-like growths. It does not cause the flesh to rot, but the whole fruit gradually becomes mummified. Sometimes the apples fall to the ground where they gradually rot and are eaten by birds and slugs, or remain on the tree during the winter.

Infection may be started at wounds made in various ways either by the weather, nail bruises, splits due to wet weather, etc., by pests such as wasps, and the larvae (small caterpillar-like insects) of Codling Moth and Apple Sawfly.

Careless handling at the time of picking or storing causes bruises and punctures in the skin help to spread the disease. In store stomes the apples turn quite black – and if kept too moist the fungus appears as a white fluff and spreads the disease to the surrounding fruits. *Control Measures* Spraying with fungicides against this disease has not been found to give good results unless applied prior to harvesting. Use then – Captan 3 weeks and 4 days before picking. The following instructions with regard to hygiene and the like should be followed:

(1) Wasps' nests in the neighbourhood should be destroyed, by putting a handful of derris dust on each hole.

(2) All over-wintering sources of infection should be destroyed by early spring. See that all mummified fruits are removed and destroyed or buried very deeply in the

ground, and cut off or burn all infected branches and spurs.

(3) A constant watch should be kept on the crop, and all infected fruits thrown into the alleyways (not under the trees) so that they can be rendered harmless. At the time of picking rotten fruit should be taken off the trees and it can then be dug into the ground during the winter.

(4) Some method of bird scaring should be adopted.

(5) Apple Scab, Codling Moth and Sawfly should be controlled by their respective methods.

(6) Do not store fruit picked without stalks or bruised or injured in any form; they may be carrying some infection which would spread amongst the other fruit.

(7) Similar methods apply to plum trees. This is most important, as after a bumper crop plum trees carry lots of mummified fruit.

(8) Do not neglect anything, and gardeners are asked to help one another as far as possible for the Brown Rot spores can be carried in the air by the wind, and can be spread rapidly from garden to garden.

Brown rot of apple. Pick off and burn affected apple

FIRE BLIGHT

Fire blight, a disease of apple and pear, is caused by the bacterium *Erwinia amylovora*.

Most pear varieties, including *Conference*, escape infection in most years, but in years of unusually high temperatures at spring blossoming time, losses can be high.

In strong growing pear trees, infected blossoms and shoots wilt and turn dark brown or black. During summer, the disease spreads rapidly through the fruiting spurs or shoots into the branches, which are quickly killed.

The first symptoms in the orchard are dead blossoms and dark leaves hanging from a truss or branch; these are seen from July onwards. The bark of diseased areas on branches is dark green or dark brown, water soaked and with an indistinct margin between healthy and infected tissue. Leaves on affected branches turn dark brown and, like infected fruits, usually remain attached to the tree after leaf fall.

In autumn the disease becomes dormant, canker extension ceases and cracks appear especially on the branches at the margin between diseased and healthy bark. The cankers may continue to extend and exude slime even in mid winter.

In less vigorous trees the symptoms are similar but the disease spreads more slowly.

Symptoms in apples are generally similar to pears, but the disease spreads more slowly. Shoot infection is characteristic: the tips wilt and droop and golden droplets of bacterial ooze are seen on the infected stem. *The Natural Spread* During warm, humid weather, diseased parts of branches exude a bacterial slime which is carried to blossoms by insects or by the splash of rain. The bacteria multiply rapidly in the blossom and are then carried to other blossoms by pollinating insects or they are infected by wind-borne contaminated pollen. The bacteria then move through the tissues of the blossoms into the fruiting spurs and so invade the branches. Branches can also be infected directly through open wounds, by slime carried from cankers. Transmission between soft shoots by insects is possible and bacteria may also invade such shoots.

Spread in the orchards during the spring has been unimportant because the temperatures during the main blossom periods are too low for spread. The pear, *Laxton's Superb* produces far more summer blossom than others; therefore *Laxton's Superb* itself is much more likely than others to become infected.

Contaminated secateurs are known to have caused the spread in some orchards.

Some of the infection seen in apple orchards has been

related to an infected hawthorn hedge. *There are other hosts* The most common hosts are pear, apple, hawthorn, Cotoneaster spp. white-beam and *Pyracantha* spp. as well as other pome fruits hosts such as rowan. *Stranvaesia davidiana*, ornamental apples and pears and quince have, however, been less commonly affected. *Control Measures* The Fire Blight Disease Order (1960) requires that any known or suspected instances of fire blight in England and Wales must be reported to the Ministry of Agriculture.

In Scotland and Northern Ireland anyone who suspects a case of fire blight is advised to report it to Plant Health Branch, Department of Agriculture and Fisheries for Scotland, Chesser House, Gorgie Road, Edinburgh, or the Department of Agriculture, Northern Ireland, Dundonald House, Upper Newtownard's Road, Belfast BT4 3SB, respectively.

All pruning implements should be disinfected in 3 per cent Lysol between use on one (presumed) healthy tree and the next.

Pruning wounds should be covered with best quality white lead paint.

All hawthorns in the vicinity of pear and apple orchards should be cut back to reduce blossoming.

Any practice that encourages soft, sappy growth should be avoided. Pruning should be kept to a minimum and spring applications of organic nitrogenous fertilisers replaced by autumn applications.

Irrigation should not be used in early summer (mid May to mid June) because it increases shoot growth; water applied during mid July to mid August aids fruit swelling without markedly increasing shoot growth. If the severity of fire blight attacks increases it may be worth reducing plant growth rates by limiting the area around trees that is treated with herbicides and thus allowing grass sward to be established closer to the base of the trees. There is limited observational evidence that the use of the growth regulator N-dimethyl-aminosuccinamic acid (available to use on apples in the formulation 'Alar') makes apple trees less susceptible to infection.

In the long term, it is advisable to replace hawthorn hedges with a suitable non-susceptible hedge – alder has been used successfully.

Growers are strongly advised to grub or topwork the variety

Laxton's Superb in areas where they are not required by law to do so. *Measures after Infection* If fire blight has been found in an orchard, attempts to eliminate the disease should be started immediately. If cutting out is permitted, it should be done within hours, preferably after the procedure has been demonstrated by a NAAS Adviser or a Plant Health Inspector. Delay will allow the organism to progress further into the tree and also allow a source of infection for healthy trees to persist longer than necessary.

If death of part of a tree is thought to be due to fire blight, a slanting cut should be made into the bark of the twig or branch well below the external signs of the disease. Continue making further cuts towards the canker or discoloured part to determine whether the reddish brown to brown staining of the bark that is typical of fire blight is present.

The tree should be grubbed if the bark of the trunk is stained, or if staining is present within 2 ft of the trunk in a branch more than 1 in. in diameter.

Twigs or shoots that are 1 in. or less in diameter and show symptoms should be cut off not less than 1 ft below the stain within the bark. Affected branches 1 in. or more in diameter should be cut off not less than 2 ft below the stain within the bark.

If three or more strikes (points of infection) are seen on a pear tree, it is advisable to grub it. Generally, more strikes than had been visible when the first were seen are likely to appear on the tree later. Present information suggests that since progress of the disease is slower in apple, cutting out will be successful and grubbing usually unnecessary.

Knives and other small implements should be disinfected in 3 per cent lysol between examining one twig or branch and the next. Saw blades that have been used to remove an infected branch should be disinfected by swabbing thoroughly with 3 per cent lysol so that not only is the blade wetted but all sawdust is removed from the teeth.

All cut surfaces remaining on the tree should be painted with best quality white lead finishing paint immediately after cutting.

In almost all cases infection will have entered the orchards from near-by infected hawthorn. A determined effort should be made to find this infection and destroy it.

In the USA spraying just before bud burst, and while the tree is still dormant, with 0.5 per cent copper sulphate of a 12-

12-100 Bordeaux mixture is advised in order to reduce the amount of infectious ooze produced in the spring.

PHYSIOLOGICAL DISEASES

BITTER PIT
The exact cause of this disorder is not known though it is thought to be a Calcium deficiency or imbalance caused by excess Potash. It may develop whilst the fruit is still on the tree, showing as dark spots underneath the skin. Later, usually in the store, the spots become sunken pits and are also scattered through the flesh.

Bitter Pit is influenced by climatic and cultural conditions which encourage vigorous growth. It is induced by heavy pruning and is found to be most prevalent on young, vigorous trees. Where there are extreme periods of heat and cold, of draught and rainfall during the season, Bitter Pit is noticeably much more prevalent. *Control Measures* Heavy pruning should be avoided and any excess applications of nitrogenous manures, as these are a stimulant to vigorous growth. Do not pick the fruit before it is ripe. Avoid heavy doses of potash. Spray the leaves of the trees with liquid seaweed in hard water in the summer. Add 1 oz of calcium chloride to 2 gals. water – if soft water has to be used.

RUBBERY WOOD
A disease known as Rubbery Wood has been noticed on many apple trees, particularly *Lord Lambourne, James Grieve, Millers' Seedling* and the *Dartmouth Crab*. The branches become flexible so that they can be bent with ease, hence the term, rubbery wood. The boughs always bend downwards with the slightest crop of fruit and very often the apples produced are very small.

The cause of this disease is not known, but it is probably a virus disease and is infectious. Graft wood should never be taken from a tree showing this trouble. It can be transmitted by secateurs when pruning or even by root contact in the soil.

WATER CORE OR GLASSINESS
In the early stages this may be seen only when the apple is cut open and the flesh around the core has a water-soaked appearance. Later on this extends outwards to the surface, appearing as glassy areas on the skin. Water or cell sap collects between the cells of the flesh, giving this watery, glassy effect.

Young trees just coming into bearing are most subject to this disorder especially if given a lot of nitrogenous manure. Again, extremes of much or little rainfall seem to bring on this glassiness, and also a high temperature, the side of the fruit in the shade being less susceptible than that in the sun.

The variety Rival is particularly prone to this disorder. *Control Measures* No really satisfactory method has been found for dealing with water core. Heavy manuring with nitrogenous manures should be avoided unless the first two or three crops are to be sacrificed to build up the framework of the tree.

If the disease is observed the fruit is on the tree, pick at once and put into store. Often the glassiness will disappear if the store is cool and well ventilated. Try and reduce stress in hot weather, ie by spraying with mist nozzles and giving a foliai feed in the water thus used.

CHAT FRUIT
This disease is sometimes associated with Rubbery Wood, but sometimes the trouble may be on its own. The fruits remain generally about $1\frac{1}{2}$ in. in diameter, and they ripen and fall early.

The trouble is suspected as being due to virus infection and no cure at present is known. So remove and burn the infected tree.

Blackberry

BLACKBERRY DWARF OR REVERSION
This is suspected to be a virus disease and is serious in cultivated blackberries. The chief symptom is that numerous stunted shoots are produced giving a witches' broom effect. The leaves are often distorted and covered with mosaic mottling. The *Cut Leaf* and *Himalayan Giant* seem to be the most susceptible varieties. It has been known to attack the *Lowberry, Phenomenal Berry* and *Youngberry. Control Measures* Dig up and burn diseased shoots at once as they are useless and a source of infection to other shoots.

Cherry

BACTERIAL CANKER (*Pseudomonas mors-prunorum* and *P. prunicola*)
When twigs and branches 'die-back' in cherry trees, the cause

may usually be attributed to attacks by the bacteria mentioned above, the former being the most commonly found. The symptoms are very similar to those found on a plum tree.

The attack may be very serious on young trees, the whole stem being girdled by the canker and so destroyed, but in cherries it is separate branches which are usually attacked, and buds and twigs are often killed.

Infection takes place during the autumn, the organism entering the tree by any wound on the stem or branches. It destroys the bark and wood and so upsets the food conductive system of the tree, the leaves of the infected branch being yellow, and unhealthy looking, and often curling upwards. Later they become withered and brown. The cankers are sunken, cracked areas on the bark, from which a great deal of gum exudes.

Amber, Bigarreau, Bigarreau de Schrecken, Bradbourne Black, Emperor Francis, Napoleon and Waterloo are among the more susceptible varieties.

Early Rivers, Frogmore, Grosvenor Wood and *Round Heart* are some of the most resistant. *Control Measures* Any pruning or cutting back of the trees should be done by the end of August or not till the following April, as any wounds or injuries to the tree during the autumn should be avoided as it is then that infection most readily takes place.

Spray with Bordeaux mixture, formula 1 lb. copper sulphate, $1\frac{1}{4}$ lb. garden lime to 17 gal. water, just before the blossoms open, and give a further spraying with Bordeaux mixture at petal fall, this time the formula being 1 lb. copper sulphate to $1\frac{1}{2}$ lb. quicklime to 25 gal. water. Spray thoroughly also just before leaf fall, using a stronger Bordeaux mixture, i.e. 1 lb. copper sulphate, $1\frac{1}{2}$ lb. quicklime to 10 gal. water. Some stocks are resistant and the high working of the bud or graft keep it off the scion.

There is evidence to show that the disease is introduced into orchards on nursery trees, and nurserymen must realise the importance of sending out young trees free from the trouble.

SILVER LEAF (*Stereum purpureum*)
This disease attacks both the sweet and acid cherries, *Napoleon* and *Turkey Heart* being the most susceptible of the sweet cherries and *Morello* of the acid cherries.

The cherry is not as badly attacked, however, by the disease as the plum. Full directions for recognising and controlling silver leaf will be found on page 146.

CHERRY LEAF SCORCH (*Gnomonia erythrostoma*)
This disease occurs on the leaves of the cherry, and Nature has cleverly arranged that the fungus attacks the tissue at the base of the leaf stalk which should separate it from the twig at leaf-fall time, thus preventing this happening and so the withered leaves stay on the tree bearing the spores of the fungus which immediately infect the young leaves when they appear in spring.

The 'scorch' starts as yellow patches on the leaves, turning brown later; as the leaves of the tree die its vigour is greatly reduced. The fruit is also attacked sometimes, and hard black spots appear in the flesh.

Two very resistant varieties are *Napoleon* and *Turkey Heart*. Some of the least resistant are *Early Amber, Frogmore, Bigarreau* and *Waterloo*. Wild cherry trees are often attacked and serve as a source of infection. *Control Measures* Gather all withered leaves from the trees and burn them. This is most necessary when young trees have been attacked, but impracticable on large standard trees, so spray these with Bordeaux mixture 6–6–100 (6 lb. quicklime, 6 lb. copper sulphate to 100 gal. water) just as the leaves are unfolding and again when the petals have fallen.

Sometimes in addition to the leaf scorch there is intervenal yellowing of the leaves. The cure here is to spray the trees with 4 per cent manganese solution of manganese sulphate in February, or to inject into the trunks of the trees solid manganese sulphate in the form of tablets, specially made for the purpose, which can now be purchased from some chemists.

BLOSSOM WILT (*Sclerotinia laxa*)
Both sweet and acid cherries may be seriously damaged by this disease. In the sweet cherry, where the flowers are borne on short spurs along the branch, all the flowers and leaves may die without actually showing canker or die back of the branch. In the *Morello* cherry, where the flowers grow directly off the slender twigs, the fungus penetrates into these causing them to die back and so the whole twigs are destroyed.

It is the most serious disease of *Morello* cherries and if the in-fection is very bad the whole tree looks as if it has been caught in a flame and burned.

The flowers may be infected before they are opened, and wither in the bud. These damaged flower buds are very conspicuous when the trees are in full flower. Infection takes place also when the flower is open and this is followed by a dying-back of the shoots bearing these infected flowers. *Control Measures* The chief method of control is to remove all the parts which have been infected as soon as they are apparent. This should be strictly done on a *Morello* which is usually grown as standards, should be sprayed with Bordeaux mixture 6–6–100 or lime-sulphur at 1 in 30 to 1 in 50.

The *Morello* cherry is very susceptible to damage caused by the lime-sulphur, so always use Bordeaux mixture on this variety.

BROWN ROT (*Sclerotinia fructigena* and *S. laxa*)
The relation of this disease to Blossom Wilt has already been pointed out in the section on Plum Rot. The same fungus which causes Wilt spreads to the fruit and causes it to rot. In the case of the cherry, *S. fructigena* also causes considerable damage later in the season, especially if the fruit is cracked and the weather wet. Both these conditions aid easy infection. *Control Measures* See Blossom Wilt. Winter spray in December with tar oil.

Currants

REVERSION
Reversion is classified as a 'virus' disease which is caused neither by bacteria nor fungi, and about which little is known as has been pointed out in the section on Plum Rot. The disease can be transmitted when a healthy bush is grafted with a shoot from an infected bush, and also a 'mite' *Eriophyes ribis*, which causes Big Bud, carries this disease from bush to bush.

As the name suggests, the bushes attacked seem to revert to a wild state, the leaves becoming smaller and darker green than in normal bushes, and the fruit-bearing capacity of the bush is impaired.

True Reversion can be seen if leaves growing from the middle portion of a vigorous shoot are examined, and it is found there are less than five side veins coming from the big mid-vein. A normal leaf has five main veins going to each five points. They are seen more easily on the underside of the leaf during the month of June.

It is important to examine leaves from a vigorous shoot, as sometimes lower branches which have been damaged or cut back hard produce leaves with fewer veins. This is known as False Reversion and such bushes later produce normal leaves, whilst those attacked by the true Reversion produce more and more abnormal leaves.

The flowers of a reverted bush are darker in colour. *Control Measures* Dig up and burn all bushes showing signs of Reversion in the winter. Never take cuttings from a bush showing any Reversion at all, even though the young shoots are normal.

Keep Big Bud mite controlled by spraying with lime-sulphur, 1 in 20, just before the flowers open. If the attack is only slight 1 in 50 will be strong enough.

CORAL SPOT (*Nectria cinnabarina*)

During the summer the wood of currant bushes may be studded with pinkish spots, hence the name 'Coral Spot'. These are signs that the bush has been attacked by the fungus *Nectria cinnabarina* which permeates the conductive tissue in the bark and wood, and causes the bush to show signs of wilting and the leaves fall from the branches so infected. The fungus lives in dead wood first of all, usually old pruning stumps, and afterwards spreads to the living branch. *Control Measures* Cut out all dead and dying branches, if possible, before the Coral Spots appear, as from these come the spores by which the disease is spread farther.

LEAF SPOT (*Pseudopeziza* and *Glaesporium ribis*)

Small dark-brown irregular shaped spots may be seen on both black and redcurrant leaves, usually about the middle of June. From these spots small cushions arise, bearing spores which become shining and sticky in wet weather, and these are splashed by the rain or carried by insects to other leaves and so the disease spreads. Severe leaf fall may occur at the end of June or the beginning of July and this causes the fruit to shrivel before it is ripe, but should this not occur, the early leaf-fall seriously affects the next year's crop. This stage of the disease is known as *Glaesporium ribis*; a further stage caused by *Pseudopeziza ribis* develops in the fallen leaves and bears spores which are dispersed into the air and are a source of infection of the new young leaves in the spring.

Of the blackcurrants, *Baldwin*, *Boskoop Giant* and *Seabrooke's*

Black are the most susceptible varieties and those not so susceptible are *Edna, Goliath, September Black* and *Victoria*.

Of the redcurrants, *Fay's Prolific* and *Fertility* are very susceptible and may suffer a great loss of vigour owing to early leaf-fall. Earliest of *Four Lands* and *La Constante* are two of the least susceptible. *Control Measures* The most effective control is to spray with Bordeaux mixture at 8–8–100 (8 lb. copper sulphate; 8 lb. quicklime to 100 gal. water and *pro rata*) in May and June, but as the deposit left on the fruit makes it unsaleable, this is only to be recommended for young stock in nursery beds. Bushes sprayed directly after the fruit is picked will have leaf fall checked and the disease will be prevented from spreading.

In gardens and small plots, the fallen leaves should be collected and burnt. In large plantations the soil should be cultivated so that the old leaves are well buried before the young leaves open the next spring.

Bushes which are lightly manured have shown themselves to be more susceptible to this disease, so a good dressing of manure is recommended to assist resistance.

CURRANT RUST (*Cronartium ribicola*)

On the undersides of the currant leaves small yellowish cushions may be seen early in the year. Later, usually after the fruit is picked, the leaves become brown and withered, turning almost black in wet weather, and the under side of the leaf is covered with coarse woolly hairs which are the second type of spore produced from the fungus which attacks, not the currant, but 'five needled pines', the fungus developing on these and producing other spores which again attack the currants. The disease is spread during the summer on the currants by spores from the yellowish cushions or 'rust' spots. *Control Measures* Avoid planting currants near *Weymouth* Pines and other five-needled pines. Spray with Bordeaux mixture as recommended for Leaf-spot.

EUROPEAN MILDEW (*Microsphaera grossulariae*)

This disease has been found on both black and redcurrants, and in the latter case has been severe enough to cause early leaf-fall, but it is more commonly found on gooseberries. The leaves show white powdery patches. *Control Measures* Full details for the control of this disease are given for Gooseberry Mildew and the same methods are recommended for currants.

AMERICAN MILDEW (*Spareotheca mors-uvae*)
Red, white and black currants are attacked by this disease, though it is found to be most destructive on gooseberries.

White powdery patches are seen on the under-surface of the leaves which are distorted and curl upwards. The mildew patches spread to the fruit, the black spots seen in these patches are the spore-bearing structure of the fungus. *Control Measures* See American Gooseberry Mildew.

CLUSTER CUPS (*Puccini Pringsheimiana*)
These bright red and orange 'cups' are tiny round blotches which may be found on the fruit and leaves and sometimes young shoots of currant bushes, but it is not a common disease. *Control Measures* See Cluster Cup Rust of **Gooseberry.**

RUNNING OFF
When the young berries, especially those towards the top of the bunch, fall off at the end of May or the beginning of June this is called 'Running off'. It can be serious enough to cause the loss of half the crop. This falling off of the young berries is due to poor pollination, caused by adverse weather conditions such as frost. If odd bushes among many fruitful bushes show this disorder, it is likely they are not the true variety, or 'rogues' as they are called, or even reverted specimens. *Control Measures* Plant the bushes in sunny sheltered positions which encourage good pollination. A beehive placed in the vicinity will of course also help!

Gooseberry

AMERICAN GOOSEBERRY MILDEW (*Sphaerotheca mors-uvae*)
This disease is the most serious one attacking gooseberries and, as the name suggests, was imported from America and first seen over here at the beginning of the century. It has been known to cause great loss in gooseberry plantations, but recently the attacks have not been so severe, owing to the precautionary measures taken to prevent the spreading of the fungus. The disease also attacks currants but is rarely very serious in its effects on these fruits.

The disease is first seen as powdery white patches on the young leaves spreading later to the fruit, these patches producing spores which spread the disease rapidly, whole shoots being stunted and deformed. Later a dark felt layer is seen on the fruits and shoots and in this black dots, by which means the fungus passes the winter, these spore cases bursting in the spring and shooting up the spores to attack the young leaves and shoots. Those branches nearest to the ground often show disease first in the spring as the spore cases fall to the ground in the autumn as well as some remaining on the twig. *Control Measures* Attention must be paid to methods of cultivation as this disease is usually found to be worse on bushes grown on moist porous soils, which have been heavily manured.

Give plenty of space for free circulation of air round the bushes. Prune to keep the centres of the bushes open and the shoots evenly spaced. Do not give heavy dressings of nitrogenous manures such as stable manure and pig manure, as the encourage soft, sappy growth, which is far more liable to become mildewed. When nitrogenous manures are given they should be applied with bone meal and potash in the form of wood ashes to counteract the tendency to form soft and sappy growth.

Any mildewed shoot tips should be cut out towards the end of August or in September before the black spore cases have fallen to the ground, but if done earlier, late sappy growth may give rise to shoots liable to be attacked by the disease.

The other method of control is by spraying with lime-sulphur, except on sulphur-shy varieties such as *Yellow Rough* and *Leveller*. On these a washing soda and soap spray should be used.

Spray with lime-sulphur, 1 gal. in 20 gal. water, before the bushes flower; again soon after the fruit has set, and again about three weeks after. Colloidal sulphur can be used for the last spraying as there is no deposit left on the fruit.

If the varieties are known to be sulphur-shy, use 1 gal. in 60 gal. water, or even 1 in 100.

A spray made up of 2 lb. washing soda and 1 lb. soft soap to 10 gal. of water may be used on all varieties, but must be used more frequently than lime-sulphur as it is more easily washed off by rain. The first spraying should be after the fruit has set, then at fortnightly intervals. Always spray in dull cloudy weather if possible, as on hot sunny days more damage is likely to be caused.

The varieties known to suffer little or no damage from sulphur sprays are *Gunner's Seedling, Howard's Lancer, May Duke* and *Whinham's Industry*.

EUROPEAN GOOSEBERRY MILDEW (*Microphaera grossulariae*)

This disease is not nearly so serious as the American Gooseberry Mildew with which it is often confused but from which it is really easily distinguishable. It occurs as powdery patches on the upper surfaces of the leaves which are not as white as in the case of American Gooseberry Mildew and rarely on the under-surface of the leaves and more rarely still on the fruit.

The means of spreading the fungi is by spores from the white patches of mildew and by over-wintering in the black spore cases, which fall to the ground and cause infection in the spring. *Control Measures* Prune the bushes to let in light and air. Shade and stagnant air are conducive to the disease. If the attack is severe and threatens to cause considerable leaf fall, dust with flowers of sulphur, or spray with lime-sulphur as directed for American Gooseberry Mildew.

GOOSEBERRY LEAF SPOT (*Pseudopeziza ribis*)

The chief damage caused by this disease is the premature leaf all resulting from an attack, but the fungus has been found on the fruit stalks and the fruits themselves.

First of all dark spots are seen on the leaves, then they turn yellow and the leaves drop off. The vigour of the tree is severely reduced if the attack is heavy. *Control Measures* Employ measures similar to those recommended for Blackcurrant Leaf Spot.

CLUSTER CUP RUST (*Puccinia pringsheimiana*)

This fungus chiefly attacks the fruit and may be seen as bright red or orange blotches on the berries. It may also be found on the leaves, and occasionally on the shoots. The cups produce yellow spores which do not infect the gooseberries further, but attack sedges and cause a 'rust' on them, which in turn produces more spores which attack the young gooseberry fruit and leaves in the spring. *Control Measures* Root up all the sedges near the bushes. Good drainage and clean cultivation should keep them out of the plantation itself.

The bushes may be sprayed with Bordeaux mixture or colloidal copper, a fortnight before the flowers open.

Loganberry

CANESPOT OR ANTHRACNOSE (*Elsinoe veneta*)
This disease is caused by the same fungus as that which attacks the raspberry. The symptoms are the same – purple spots with white centres appearing on stems and leaves and flower stalks. The fruit is small and unevenly developed as in the raspberry. The spots on the canes turn into sunken cankers and some of the buds on these canes do not develop. A number of the flowers do not set fruit and the development of the fruit is poor and so is the plant; the crop is adversely affected. It is perhaps the most serious disease of the loganberry. *Control Measures* By training the young canes above the fruiting canes, risk of infection by the rain splashing spores from the old canes on to the young canes is lessened.

Spray with Bordeaux mixture 2–2–50 (2 lb. copper sulphate, 2 lb. quicklime per 50 gal. water and *pro rata*) before the flowers open and again after the blossoms fall at the end of June. Colloidal copper may be used for later spray as it leaves no deposit on the fruits, and derris may be added to control the Loganberry Beetle, using $\frac{1}{2}$ lb. derris, $\frac{1}{2}$ pt colloidal copper, $\frac{3}{4}$ lb. soap and 25 gal. water.

Peach and nectarine

PEACH LEAF CURL (*Taphrina deformans*)
Peach, Nectarine and Almond trees grown in the open are most susceptible to this disease. Those grown under glass are less frequently attacked.

The symptoms are outstanding – the leaves being curled up and turning pinky red in the later stages, and finally falling to the ground and causing defoliation and a severe reduction in vigour. Sometimes new leaves develop towards the end of the season, but the quantity and quality of the fruit are very much affected.

It is thought that the spores of the fungus winter in the bud scales and not in the young shoots, and these spores attack the young leaves directly they open, causing them to become smaller and curled, and generally distorted, being a pale greenish yellow at first, then more swollen and turning a reddish colour. The infection spreads from the leaves to the young shoots, which also become distorted, and the disease may spread to the flowers and fruit. *Control Measures* Cut out infected shoots and remove and burn infected leaves as soon as they are apparent.

To ensure a good control, spray the tree just before the buds begin to swell, towards the end of February, using either 1 pt of lime-sulphur solution in 29 pts of water (1 in 30) or Bordeaux mixture at 4-4-50, which is mixed as follows: 11 gal. water, 1 lb. quicklime, $\frac{1}{2}$ lb. copper sulphate. The Royal Horticultural Society recommends spraying with Burgundy mixture made as follows: $9\frac{3}{4}$ oz. copper sulphate, 11 oz. sodium carbonate in 3 gal. water.

If the attack is very severe an autumn application of wash after the leaves have fallen is found to be helpful. *The Garlic Method* Plant cloves of garlic under the branches all around the trees or bushes three feet away from the main stem. Plant 2 ft apart and 2 in. deep in a big circle. Do the planting in November. If against a wall, a semi-circle 1 ft away is better, and plant parallel to the trained laterals. *Foliar Feeds* It has been found that to spray the leaves in June with a seaweed foliar feed helps greatly to keep the trees healthy.

MILDEW (*Sphaerotheca pannosa*)
Powdery patches on the leaves and young shoots are a sign that the tree is suffering from mildew. The growth of the shoot becomes stunted and the leaves narrow and deformed. The white powdery appearance of the infected parts is due to the spores formed by the fungus. These spread the disease to other leaves and shoots, but the fungi live through the winter in the form of mycelium composed of thin, thread-like structures in the younger shoots. *Control Measures* Cut out all infected shoots. Spray with lime-sulphur at the rate of 1 in 120 (1 pt lime-sulphur in 15 gal. water). Garlic also helps as in Leaf Curl.

SHOT-HOLE (*Clasterosporium carpophilium*)
The shot-hole effect found on peach leaves first starts as brown spots on the leaves the centre of which fall out having been killed by the fungus. Not only are the leaves attacked, but the fruits and young twigs may become infected, scabs and gum being produced on them. This disease can cause serious damage in an orchard. *Control Measures* Just as the buds begin to swell, spray with Bordeaux Mixture, 1 lb. quicklime, 1 lb. copper sulphate to 11 gal. water, or 1 pt of lime-sulphur in $3\frac{1}{2}$ gal. of water.

Spray again with lime-sulphur at the rate of 1 pt to $6\frac{1}{4}$ gal. when the flower buds show pink, and again after petals have fallen, with 1 pt lime-sulphur in $18\frac{1}{2}$ gal. water. Only if the attack was severe the previous season are these last two applications necessary.

Occasionally a leaf spot occurs which is followed by 'shot-hole' and this is thought to be due to unfavourable soil cultural conditions, and care should be taken to keep the trees growing healthily by seeing that they have enough water, but are never water-logged and also by manuring them well.

CHLOROSIS

This disease is a discoloration of the foliage, the leaves being a pale, yellowish green, caused by a lack of iron in the tree. There may be no iron shortage in the soil, but an excess of other substances which prevents the roots from absorbing the iron.

To find out if the discoloration of the leaves is due to chlorosis, cut off the tip of a leaf on a shoot bearing these pale leaves and bend the shoot over so that the cut surface of the leaf is immersed in a receptacle. This should contain a 0.1 per cent solution of iron citrate. Leave the shoot there for 18 hours, and after that time should the leaf become the usual green colour, it shows that the discoloration is due to lack of iron.

It is important that leaves should be a good green colour, as this shows that the tissues are able to carry out their function of manufacturing the food required by the plant. *Control Measures* Excess of lime in the soil is conducive to chlorosis, so heavy dressings of lime and phosphates should be avoided but dressings of well prepared compost or any old organic manures are recommended. A green crop, such as mustard or rape, can be grown and forked in.

Iron sequestrols may be diluted with water in accordance with the instructions on the bottle. This solution should be watered liberally around the affected tree or bush.

Pills containing exactly the right proportions of iron to correct the deficiency may be pushed into the trunks of trees. Holes are made with brace and bit and the pills are pushed in with a pill pusher.

SPLIT STONE

When peaches are cracked towards the stalk end, if the fruit is cut open it is found that the stone is split and the kernel rotting. Sometimes earwigs or other insects have got in, and the brownish substance 'frass' is seen.

The splitting may be due to inefficient pollination, but more likely to a deficiency of lime in the soil, so a dressing of lime is to be recommended.

Pear

PEAR CANKER (*Nectria galligena*)

Some varieties of pears are most susceptible to this disease as in the case of apples, the same fungus being the cause of the trouble. It is most serious if not controlled. The symptoms are the same as in apple canker, the fungus entering by scab wounds in the same way and producing the same swollen distorted conditions – attacking both twigs and branches, and if left uncontrolled will spread and eventually kill the tree.

In summer white 'strings' appear in the canker, giving rise to spores and so spreading the disease, and on the older cankers, dark red egg-like growths are seen which again help to spread the disease. Most susceptible varieties are *Fertility* and *Marie Louise*. *Control Measures* Cut back any badly infected branch to well below the canker and any wood that is discoloured. Cut out all infected shoots. Burn all prunings and paint all cut surfaces with white lead paint. Grow trees as bushes rather than as standards so that spraying against Scab and the pruning out of diseased portions can be done easily and thoroughly.

PEAR SCAB (*Venturia pirina*)

The fungus causing pear scab is a different species from that causing apple scab, but they are very much alike to look at and in their ways of attacking and spreading over a tree, young shoots, leaves and fruit. The fungus winters in cracks on the shoots and on dead fallen leaves. In spring spores are produced, and the young leaves and flowers become immediately infected and the scabs caused on these in time produce more spores and so further infection is caused.

Some of the most susceptible varieties are *Beurré Bosc, Beurré Clairgeau, Beurré d'Amanlis, Clapp's Favourite, Doyenné du Comice, Marie Louise* and *William Bon Chrétien. Conference* and *Dr Julyes Guyot* are also susceptible varieties. *Control Measures* Prune out all scabbed twigs before the spring and burn them. Rake together all old leaves and burn them. Spray as in the case of

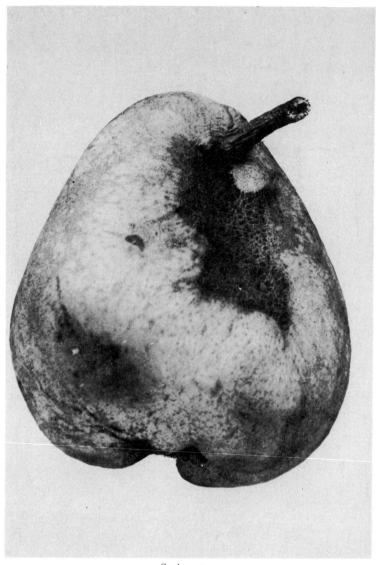

Scab on pears

apples – at green bud, pink bud, petal-fall and two or three weeks after.

As a rule Bordeaux mixture is preferred to lime-sulphur, and can generally be used without harming the pears.

Bordeaux mixture used at the strength of 8-8-100 is made as

follows: 8 lb. copper sulphate, 8 lb. quicklime to 100 gal. water and *pro rata*.

If this strength causes too much russeting on the fruit, reduce to 6-6-100 or 4-4-100.

If using lime-sulphur, do so at $2\frac{1}{2}$ per cent for pre-blossom spraying but only at 1 per cent blossom – but at this dilution it is not as effective as Bordeaux mixture.

STONY PIT or DIMPLED PEARS
This is a virus that curiously distorts and dimples the fruits. They may be covered with deep irregularly shaped pits at the base of which are quite hard cells. The bases of the pits are usually dark green and the raised portions paler. The pears are smaller than normal and the fruit may fall prematurely. The trees become useless and the fruit is unfit for sale or for home consumption. The following varieties are very subject to this trouble: *Doyenné du Comice*, *Pitmaston Duchess* and *Durondeau*, *Beaurré Bedford* and *Laxton's Superb*.

The trees with this disease are unlikely to recover, and so they should be removed and burned. Graft wood should never be taken from such trees.

Plum

BACTERIAL CANKER (*Pseudomonas mors-prunorum*)
This can be a serious disease of plums, causing up to 2 per cent loss of trees in a young orchard.

The symptoms of the disease are stunted shoots, and yellowing leaves which wither later in the season. The disease enters the stem and branches through some wound on the surface, kills the bark and young wood, and produces the effects described above. If the canker girdles the whole branch it dies. The organisms which spread the disease usually die early in the summer and if the branches are not girdled completely, the canker heals, and the branches eventually recover. The disease also attacks the leaves, forming small round spots which turn brown, and the centre falls out causing a 'shot-like' effect. *Control Measures* Avoid injuring stems and branches and causing wounds by which the bacteria can enter. As the infection occurs most readily in October, November and December, all pruning and cutting out of branches should be done by the end of August or left until the following April.

Spray with a Bordeaux mixture using 1 lb. copper sulphate,

$1\frac{1}{2}$ lb. quicklime to 25 gal. water. It is said the inclusion of a little cotton-seed oil in the wash diminishes the chance of spray injury. Do this three weeks after petal fall, and two weeks later spray with a colloidal copper preparation, using a strong solution.

The most susceptible varieties: *Victoria, Czar, Giant Prune, Prince of Wales* and *Bradley's King Damson.*

BRANCH DIE BACK (*Diaporthe perniciosa* and *Dermatea prunastri*)

This disease attacks plum and greenage trees which are made unhealthy either by growing on unsuitable soil or having been previously attacked by bacteria. The fungus can be seen in two stages – on dead and dying branches of a tree or in bacterial cankers (1) As tiny stiff hairs and (2) later as tiny button-shaped bodies which are soft and jelly-like in wet weather but hard and leathery in dry weather. *Control Measures* The trees should be kept as healthy as it is possible to make them by suitable manuring and cultural operations. All cankered branches should be cut out and burnt.

SILVER LEAF (*Stereum purpureum*)

The Ministry of Agriculture found it necessary to issue an order in 1923 compelling people to cut out branches infected by this fungus as the disease was becoming so serious.

It is easily recognised by the silvery appearance of the leaves, due to a layer of air just below the skin. The wood of the infected branch is stained brown, and this symptom distinguishes the disease from a silvering of the leaves due to purely physical conditions.

The varieties *Victoria* and *Czar* are most susceptible to the disease, whilst *Pershore Yellow Egg* is most resistant and shows the highest proportion of recoveries. *Control Measures* Affected branches should be cut away only when wilting occurs (as the silvery leaves themselves are not infectious) and before the branch dies as it is then that the fungus comes to the surface and forms purple bracket fungi on the dead wood, which spread the disease to other trees. The wilting branches must be cut out by 15 July according to law.

Do not prune the trees in autumn, winter or early spring, as the spores can enter through the open surfaces. If, however, it is found necessary to do so during these periods, cover the cuts with white lead paint.

Be sure to cut infected branches well down into the healthy wood as the brown stain shows where the fungus is present. Applications of fish manure or meat and bone meal at the rate of 4 oz per sq. yd are found to be helpful in keeping the tree healthy and vigorous and therefore give it a better chance to recover from the attack.

Dried blood can be used instead at 3 oz to the sq. yd all over the ground as far as the branches spread.

SHOT-HOLE and LEAF SPOT (*Pseudomonas mors-prunorum*)

This has already been mentioned in the note on bacterial canker and though the Leaf Spot is not a serious disease in itself, it must be remembered that it is the same fungus which causes the canker which can girdle the stem and so kill the tree. These 'shot-holes' are most noticeable in wet summers as the moisture helps to spread the disease. *Control Measures* Spray foliage in spring and summer with Bordeaux mixture 6-6-100 (6 lb. copper sulphate, 6 lb. quick lime to 100 gal. water). It will be necessary to spray more frequently during a wet season if the disease is very prevalent.

BLOSSOM WILT (*Sclerotinia laxa*)

The whole blossom on neglected trees may be destroyed by this disease especially if the weather is wet at the time the trees are in flower.

The fungus attacks the young shoots, causing Twig Blight, Wither Tip and Blossom Wilt and also Brown Rot of the fruit, these various names describing the effects the same fungus has on the various parts of the shoot it attacks and it is important to realise these stages are all related in producing the Brown Rot of the fruit. *Control Measures* Withered tips, blighted twigs, spurs with cankers on, and mummified fruits should all be removed from the tree and burnt. This will help to prevent further infection.

Spray with Bordeaux mixture 8-8-100 or lime-sulphur 1 in 30 just as the flowers are opening.

BROWN ROT (*Sclerotinia fructigena* and *S. laxa*)

Brown Rot is caused by attacks of one or the other of the fungi named above. Sometimes both are found on the same tree. Infection is spread from one plum to another through any puncture caused either by bruising or insects.

S. fructigena has been found to be the cause of most Brown

Rot in storage, whilst *S. laxa* as already mentioned, is responsible for Blossom Wilt. *Control Measures* Remove all mummified fruits from tree and burn. Take great care in picking the fruit which is to be placed in a cold store. It is a good thing to pick the larger fruit with the stalks on, as the disease can enter through stalk scars.

The spray programme advised under Blossom Wilt will help to control the Brown Rot of the fruit.

SOOTY BLOTCH (*Glaeodes pomigena*)

During a wet summer an attack of Sooty Blotch can be quite serious. The Blotch caused is similar to that on apples, appearing as circular brownish areas on the skin, especially on those varieties with light skins such as *Warwickshire Drooper, Pershore Egg, Victoria, Pond's Seedling Giant Prune* and *Cambridge Gage* are other varieties on which the disease has been found. *Control Measures* Avoid planting trees on a heavy, badly drained soil, and planting too thickly. Allow the trees as much light and air as possible. A post-blossom spray of 1 per cent lime-sulphur or colloidal sulphur at $\frac{1}{2}$ lb. to 10 gal. water will help to check the disease.

FRUIT GUMMING

When fruit is needed for canning or bottling it is a drawback to find the fruit swelling and cracking during the proceedings and exuding a gelatinous gum-like substance. It is present in the fruit before picking and sometimes a few drops appear as the fruit is ripening.

No direct cause which produces this gumming has yet been found. Apparently it is due to some physical disorder. *Control Measures* Thorough cultivation of the soil is very important, especially in dry weather, to encourage fruit to develop regularly when growing. On heavy soil, cultivate to encourage drainage and avoid water-logging. Mulching with any form of organic matter in December is advantageous.

PLUM POX

Plum pox is a serious virus disease, widespread on the continent. It has recently been found, however, in British nurseries. It is necessary for nurserymen to notify the Ministry of the presence of this disease under the Plum Pox (Sharka Disease) Order 1975, and they are required under the order to destroy infected trees. Plum pox is transmitted by aphids and renders the fruit unpalatable because of pigmented blotches and rings on the skin, plus reddish discoloration of the flesh beneath, often extending to the stone. Some varieties develop grey or yellowish blotches or rings on the leaves. Any suspicious symptoms must immediately be brought to the attention of the Ministry of Agriculture. Suspicious symptoms should immediately be referred to the local ADAS horticultural officer.

Raspberry

BLUE STRIPE WILT (*Verticillium dahliae*)
This disease derives its name from the blue discoloration of the cane which takes place, usually starting at the base and developing upwards along one side of the cane, the leaves on the discoloured side withering and dying. When the discoloration encircles the cane all the leaves die.

The first symptoms are seen on the leaves about the end of June. There are yellowish blotches, usually in the strips between the main veins. These strips gradually turn brown, whilst those near the vein remain green, giving the leaf a striped appearance. The lower leaves are affected first. They wither and curl inwards, exposing the white under-surface. Then they fall off, often leaving a tuft of healthy leaves at the top, or only one side of the cane may be infected and healthy leaves are left along the side which is free from infection.

No fungus is visible unless the cane is cut through the discoloured portion and examined under a microscope, and then minute black bodies are found which fall to the ground with the dead leaves and canes and attack other canes. As the infection comes mostly from the soil, the roots and underground portions of the stem are usually attacked first. *Control Measures* By good cultivation and manuring, improve the health of the canes and encourage them to grow away from the disease. If a shoot is badly infected it should be dug up completely and burnt. Cut out any dead or dying canes, collect old leaves and burn them. Never propagate from an infected shoot, as the fungus may be transferred to a clean plantation by the woody tissue of the cane itself in to the soil about its roots.

CANE BLIGHT (*Leptosphaeria coniothyrium*)
This disease can cause serious damage in a raspberry plantation if it is not recognised at an early stage and dealt with. It is

identified by the wilting and withering of the leaves; the canes become very brittle and snap off very easily just above soil level, and at the base of these canes there is an area of discoloured bark – this cracks, and shows more or less round black fruiting bodies of the fungus. *Control Measures* Cut right back to the base all diseased canes. Breaking out is no use as the infected parts are still left on the shoot, causing further infection. Do not use the same knife for thinning out strong healthy shoots, until it has been well disinfected.

Do not transplant the 'spawn' (the young rooted shoots) from a plantation where the disease has been observed, but if this has to be done, sacrifice the first year's crop by cutting off all the old canes to below the soil level so that the new canes may grow up without a chance of infection from the old.

SPUR BLIGHT (*Didymella applanata*)

In this disease the canes do not die but the buds are killed which should have developed and produced fruit, so the crop is curtailed. Dark purplish patches appear on the canes, usually at the base of the leaves. They may be 2–6 in. long, and the leaves growing on such canes are often blotched with large spots, dark brown in colour and irregular in shape.

The purplish blotches on the canes gradually lose their colour, becoming a greyish white, full of black dots which contain the spores, which are shot out when moistened by rain or dew and attack the young canes and so the disease is carried on. Wet conditions in spring and crowded plantations encourage the disease. *Control Measures* Thin the canes to avoid overcrowding. Cut out and burn all badly infected canes. If these measures do not check the disease, spray with Bordeaux mixture as recommended for Cane Spot.

CANE SPOT or ANTHRACNOSE (*Elsinoë veneta*)

At the end of May or the beginning of June, small round spots on the base of the young canes may be seen. As the canes grow, so the spots become larger and more elongated in shape. The centre of the spot turns white with a purple edge. Later the spot becomes sunken into small pits or cankers.

Canes may be infected from May to October, but the spots from the later infections do not become sunken pits, but greyish-white and develop small black dots, easily seen with a hand lens. They are the fruiting bodies of the fungus.

The leaf stalks and leaves are also attacked, showing the

same purple spots with white centre as are found on the canes. If the attack is severe the edges of the leaves curl downwards and may fall to the ground. The fungus may spread to the fruit and directly affect the quantity and quality of the crop, the fruits attacked being misshapen and one-sided, the droplets on the side attacked remaining small and green.

Blackberries and loganberries are also attacked by the same fungus.

The varieties of raspberry most immune are *Malling Promise* and *Malling Enterprise,* those most susceptible being *Lloyd George* and *Norfolk Giant. Control Measures* Badly spotted and cankered canes must be cut out and burnt. Then spray with either Bordeaux at 12-12-100 or lime-sulphur 1 in 15 when the buds on the cane are not more than half an inch out. Spray again when the flower buds are just showing white tips, with Bordeaux at 6-6-100 or lime-sulphur 1 in 40.

If propagating has to be done from infected shoots, the same procedure as advised for Cane Blight is recommended. Cut the canes back to below the ground and sacrifice the crop so that the new canes come up clean.

RASPBERRY MILDEW (*Sphaerotheca humili*)
Crowded canes and a shady situation encourage mildew. It attacks the leaves, making large white powdery patches. It is seldom serious, but does weaken the plant. When it starts to spread to the fruit it must be dealt with. *Control Measures* Dust with a fine sulphur dust. If the disease appears year after year the site where the canes are growing should be changed and a more open and sunny situation found.

RASPBERRY MOSAIC
This disorder is caused by a virus which is characterised by the mottling of the leaves, producing the same effect as mosaic. There are three types of mottling – one which covers the surface of the leaves, being only slightly sunken – if at all – and having no curling or distortion of the leaves. Another type shows yellowish patches near the edges of the leaves and between the main veins. These patches are slightly sunken and the edges of the leaves curl downwards. The third type has sharply defined yellow patches scattered over the leaf surface, these patches being deeply sunken and the whole leaf curled and distorted.

The virus penetrates the whole plant, so spawn taken from

an infected stool takes the virus with it and is diseased from the first. Stools which are infected with mosaic gradually become worse until they are dwarfed and unfruitful and a source of infection to others.

It is believed that the disease may be transmitted from infected to clean stock by the aphis *Amphorophora rubi. Control Measures* When planting new bushes be sure they are mosaic free – obtained from a reliable nursery which specialises in producing disease-free canes.

If the disease appears amongst bushes already planted, dig up and burn any stools showing bad mosaic. A new plantation should be planted not nearer than 50 ft to the diseased one, which should be dug up and burnt. As aphids are the 'vectors' of this disease see that they are controlled.

Strawberry

RED CORE DISEASE (*Phytophthora fragariae* (Hickman))
This disease is sometimes known as 'Lanarkshire Disease', as it first appeared there in 1921 but now it is found in most districts of Scotland and has spread to England as far as Devon and Cornwall.

In May and June patches of small unhealthy plants are seen. The plants may seem to recover during the summer but in the autumn they will be obvious again. The plants in the patches are small, the leaves reddish, and the outside ones may be dead.

If the plants are pulled up the roots will be found to be dead, or nearly so, there will be no fibrous roots at all, and in the centre of the blackened dead roots will be found a red portion from which the name Red Core is derived. *Control Measures* Unfortunately no control measures have proved of any use. The only known control is, therefore, to dig up the affected plants and *burn* them.

Several immune or resistant types have now been raised, the most successful being the *Auchincruive* (West of Scotland Agricultural College) varieties. There is no doubt that the disease is carried about from place to place by infected runners, and it is most important, therefore, to obtain plants from districts where the disease is absent. The disease can be carried on implements like forks and rakes.

LEAF SPOT (*Mycosphaerella fragariae*)
Small circular spots appear on the leaves, some distance apart

from each other. At first they are red, then grey and then they may be almost white with a dark red edge to them. In very severe attacks the leaves are killed. *Control Measures* After picking, set light to the straw and let it burn through the rows. If the disease seems serious in the early part of the season, spray with colloidal copper. Pick off diseased leaves and burn them. Select runners from plants free from leaf spot.

STRAWBERRY MILDEW (*Sphaerotheca humuli*)
Black blotches appear on the upper surfaces of the leaves, the under-surface being greyish in colour. The leaves later curl up.

The most susceptible varieties are *Sir Joseph Paxton* and *British Queen*. *Royal Sovereign* seems to be fairly resistant. *Control Measures* Dust with a good sulphur dust from the end of April once every ten days until the fruit starts to grow. After the fruit is picked, spray with lime-sulphur.

Formula: 1 pt to 100 pts water.

If straw is used along the rows to keep the berries clean, set light to it after the fruit is picked and so burn off a great number of old leaves.

YELLOW EDGE
This disorder is caused by a virus carried from plant to plant by aphids (greenflies). Unfortunately, symptoms do not show at once and so apparently healthy plants may produce diseased runners.

The first symptoms, however, are shown on the younger leaves which are undersized and discoloured. Gradually all the leaves are small and have yellow edges. They curl upwards, giving a cup-shaped effect and the stalks are short and stout. *Control Measures* Destroy all the plants in the garden and buy in guaranteed virus-free plants. Any plants showing Yellow Edge subsequently as a result of yellow edge infection should be dug up and burnt at once.

Give all the young plants warm-water treatment (see chapter 12) before planting.

Control aphids by spraying with nicotine and soft soap (for formula, see chapter 15). For further details, see chapter 9.

CRINKLE
A similar virus disease to Yellow Edge, but in this case, yellow spots appear all over the leaf and the foliage looks crinkled rather than curled up. In mild cases the tiny yellowish spots

will later turn reddish purple. In severe cases the spots are more numerous and later they will become brown with a yellow margin. The older leaves will be smaller than usual and the younger leaves paler in colour. *Control Measures* See Yellow Edge.

GREY MOULD ROT (*Botrytis cinerea*)
Only serious in wet weather. A grey mould-like fungus appears on the berries and the grey tufts which appear velvety ruin the fruits. *Control Measures* See that all fruits rest on the straw and not on the ground.

Let in as much light as possible by holding the leaves together off the ground with a rubber around them. These should be released after the fruit has been picked.

STRAWBERRY LEAF BLOTCH (*Gnomonia* sp)
This disease was first recorded in 1941. It causes blotches on the leaves brown with a purplish border, and outside this a yellowish zone. On dead leaf stalks another fungal form has been found as Black Spheroids.

Shady moist conditions favour the spread of this disease, and it is never advisable, therefore, to plant strawberries under such conditions. Care should be taken never to propagate infected plants.

Vine, Grape

POWDERY MILDEW (*Uncinula necator*)
One of the commonest diseases of grapes. The leaves, young shoots, flowers and fruits may be attacked both under glass and in the open. White powdery patches appear on the leaves, and these will spread to the fruit, causing it to crack and fall. *Control Measures* See that the growths are thinned out well to prevent overcrowding.

Under glass give plenty of good ventilation, plus heat, so as to ensure a buoyant atmosphere.

Paint the vine stems with a mixture of sulphur and soft soap during the winter. Dust with sulphur dust directly the powdery patches are seen.

RIPE ROT (*Glomerella cingulata*)
Swollen oblong patches appear on the fruit where later little cushions are produced. From these some a sticky substance.

The whole vine may be quickly infected from one or two diseased berries turn purple and become shrunken. *Control Measures* Cease syringing the vines directly the trouble is seen.

Give adequate ventilation. Reduce the moisture. Pick off all infected berries and *burn* them.

SUN SCALD

A trouble merely caused by variation in temperature, thus causing condensation in the house. The berries become covered with moisture and, if the hot sun strikes these drops of water the tissue below becomes scaled and dead discoloured sunken patches appear. *Control Measures* Never allow the atmosphere to be too moist. Ventilate by day and by night. Maintain a little heat in the pipes to keep the atmosphere buoyant and prevent the temperature from falling too low early in the morning.

SHANKING

A dark spot appears on the stalk of the berry. This spot increases till it encircles the stalk. The berry does not ripen. Black varieties turn red, and white varieties remain green. Both are sour. *Control Measures* Give adequate manuring to keep the vines growing. Avoid waterlogging at all costs. Do not allow the rods to overcrop or 'shanking' may appear the next season. Remove all infected berries and burn them. Do not allow overcrowding. On the other hand do not over-prune in summer.

11 The pests and diseases of lawns and ornamental trees and shrubs

Lawns

INSECT PESTS OF LAWNS

LEATHER JACKETS
For general remarks on leather jackets, see chapter 3.

They are, however, a very serious pest of lawns, eating the roots of the grasses so badly that serious browning occurs and dying, and in many cases tufts of turf can be pulled out easily by the hand. *Control Measures* The best method of controlling leather jackets on lawns seems to be to water with a special solution of ortho-dichlorobenzene with which has been mixed a proportion of Jeyes fluid. This may be obtained from the Board of Greenkeeping Research, Bingley, Yorks. $\frac{1}{4}$ gal. of the emulsion is sufficient for 100 gal. water, and the dilute solution should be used at the rate of 1 gal. per sq. yd.

Arsenate of lead powder may also be used at the rate of $\frac{1}{2}$ oz per sq. yd. This should be applied each winter during the months of November and December.

Other pests that may damage lawns are Cock-chafer Grubs (see chapter 3) and to control these it is necessary to inject carbon bi-sulphide into the soil. Special tools may be purchased for this purpose.

Watering with a strong solution of liquid derris will also control ants. (See p. 222 for further information on ANTS).

DISEASES OF LAWNS

FUSARIUM PATCH (*Fusarium nivale*)
The commonest disease of lawns today. The turf will be found attacked in September or October when unsightly brown patches will be found sometimes as small as a penny, at other times over 1 ft. in diameter. In mid conditions a cotton-like growth may appear on the surface. Infections seem to occur when the vigour of the grasses is on the decline. *Control*

Measures As generous dressings of fertilizers in the late summer encourage this disease, they should be withheld. Fertilizers rich in nitrogen seem to encourage the *fusarium*. Grass which is cut in the winter is less susceptible than lawns which are left long.

Aerate the lawn by plunging a fork held perpendicularly all over the surface.

There are several proprietary organic mercury compounds on the market, such as Verdasan, at the present time for controlling this disease.

A simple formula, however, is to mix up 2 oz finely powdered corrosive sublimate and 2 oz calomel, and apply these at the rate of 4 oz per 1,000 sq. ft of turf. To do this it is necessary to mix the chemicals with about 30 lb. of sand. This ensures even distribution.

FAIRY RINGS
These are produced by various fungi that live in the soil. They grow out from a central point, producing an ever-widening circle. *Control Measures* Make up a solution of sulphate or iron.

Formula: 1oz sulphate of iron to 1 gal. water, or water the ground concerned with a 2 per cent solution of formaldehyde, giving a thorough soaking.

RED THREAD DISEASE
Proper name *Corticium*. The patches are at first small but spread rapidly a yard or more in diameter. Usually seen in the late summer or autumn. Gardeners notice tiny thin red needles projecting from the leaves of the dead grass. *Control Measures* This is a sign of nitrogen shortage so apply dried blood at 2 oz to the sq. yd. Use a mercury dressing as advised for Fusarium Patch.

The pests of ornamental garden plants

Naturally, large numbers of the pests that attack fruit trees attack the ornamental trees and shrubs also, for so many of them are nearly related. The caterpillars, for instance, of the Lackey Moth, Vapourer Moth, Winter Moth, Ermine Moth, Tortrix Moth, will all of them be found on occasions attacking trees used for ornamental purposes and methods of control will be found in chapter 9 under the headings of **Apple, Pear** or **Cherry.**

The caterpillars that tunnel up the trunks of trees, like those of the Wood Leopard Moth, are also quite common unfortunately among ornamental trees, as are the shot-borer beetles. To eradicate these pests, the measures outlined in chapter 11 should be followed.

General advice, however, with regard to trees and shrubs may now be given. All prunings should be burnt, all dead twigs and branches removed for burning, and all wounds made painted over with a thick white lead paint. All suckers growing up from the base of trees and shrubs should be cut off below ground level the moment they are seen. Liberal dressings of nitrogenous manures such as sulphate of ammonia or nitrate of soda should never be given, as these encourage soft growth, as do over-liberal dressings of stable and farmyard manure mulchings.

The soil where the trees grow should be properly drained and deeply cultivated before planting. Badly drained soil only causes reduced vigour and this tends to make the trees susceptible to both insect and fungus attacks. All rubbish around the trees should be collected and burnt and this especially applies to shrub borders and hedgerows. By removing such material, the sources of shelter of many insects are removed.

Pests that attack numerous shrubs and trees

APHIDS (*Greenfly*)

There are a large number of species of aphids that will attack ornamental trees and shrubs. Some are black like those that attack the flowering cherries. Some are green like those that attack pyrus and prunus; some may be reddish in colour, but they all suck the sap of the leaves and stems and they all deposit what is known as 'honeydew', a sticky substance which seems to attract ants. It is on such substances that the sooty fungi grow. *Control Measures* The trees should be sprayed with either nicotine and soft soap (for formula, see chapter 13) or with liquid derris in water. Forcible spraying should be done and the whole of the shrub or tree should be covered.

Deciduous trees may be sprayed in the winter when they are dormant with a 5 per cent solution of DNOC wash.

WOOLLY APHIS (*Eriosoma lanigerum*)

For full details on woolly aphis see **Apple,** chapter 9.

It does attack the cotoneaster, the pyracantha and pyrus.

All three may be sprayed with nicotine and soft soap or with liquid derris immediately the pest is seen.

MEALY BUGS and SCALES

Mealy bugs and scales have already been described in some detail in chapter 11 under vines, etc. The Mussel Scale is dealt with in chapter 9 under **Apple.**

There are numbers of scales, however, which are found on ornamental trees and shrubs. In the case of aucubas the scale is very conspicuous, being white, and may be seen on both the upper and lower surfaces of the leaves.

The mussel scale will attack cotoneaster, ceanothus and various species of pyrus.

Carpenteria, cotoneaster, escallonia, lonicera, etc., will be attacked by the peach scale which is reddish brown and oval. This will also attack flowering currants.

Yews are often attacked by the yew scale, which is somewhat flatter and paler than the peach scale.

Elm, hazel, hawthorn, pyrus and pyracanthas may be attacked by the nut scale, which is similar again to the peach scale, except that the sides of the scale often protrude beyond the base.

Holly, myrtle and ivy are sometimes attacked by a soft scale. It is yellowy in colour, and never has a scaly covering.

Bay and laurel are sometimes attacked by a similar scale which, because of the honeydew or sticky excreta that exudes, attracts the sooty fungi which add to the disfigurement.

Beech trees can be attacked by the felted beech scale which will cover the main branches and stems. It is whitish in appearance.

Flowering currants (*rubes*) false acacias (*robinias*), laburnums and ceanothus are often attacked by mealy bugs which are similar in appearance to scale insects only their bodies are protected by a waxy white secretion rather than by scales. They can also move about plants which scales cannot. *Control Measures* In the spring, spray with white oil and nicotine.

Formula: 1 oz nicotine, 1 pt white oil petroleum emulsion to 10 gal. water. It is best to spray in the evening after a warm day.

AZALEA
(*Azalea Indica*)
The leaves and buds of azaleas may be damaged by a fungus,

Exobasidium japonicum, which attacks the terminal buds and the leaves near the tips of stems. As a result these become swollen, turn pinkish in colour and later are covered with a white bloom. *Control Measures* All affected parts should be pruned away carefully immediately the trouble is seen. They should be burnt *immediately.* It is very important to remove the trouble before the whitish bloom appears for this contains the spores which cause the spread of the disease.

CAMELLIA

A disease known as *Pestalozzia guepini* may attack camellias, causing silvery-white irregular or rounded blotches on the leaves. Minute black dots can be seen when these are examined carefully. *Control Measures* All diseased leaves should be removed and burnt directly they are seen. The remaining leaves should be sprayed with Bordeaux mixture.

As Bordeaux mixture will spot the blooms, many gardeners prefer to sponge the leaves with Bordeaux mixture instead of spraying them. This takes far more time.

LILAC

LEAF MINER

The larvae of a number of Gracilaria moths are leaf-mining. They not only injure the leaves of lilacs, but privets as well. Blisters will be found on the leaves, many of which will roll up. *Control Measures* Spray with nicotine and soft soap (for formula, see chapter 13) in May and again in July.

PRIVET

PRIVET THRIPS (*Dendothrips ornatus*)

The species is well known in the USA where it is also called the Privet Thrip and it is present also on the continent.

It was first recorded as a pest in Britain at Woking, Surrey, in August 1952.

Attacked foliage becomes silvered and in severe cases a certain amount of defoliation occurs. The eggs are inserted into the underside of leaf tissue and are found as early as the first week in April. On hatching they give rise to yellow larvae which feed on both surfaces of the leaves. The adults are about 1 mm. in length and the wings have a series of light and dark bands along them which give the insect a striped appearance.

All stages are present on the foliage in the spring and summer which suggests that there are several overlapping generations each year. By autumn adult females remain to over-winter beneath fallen leaves. *Control Measures* Spray with liquid derris or use a Pysect Aerosol.

RHODODENDRON

WHITE FLY (*Dialeurodes chittendeni*)
The leaves mottle, but no chocolate spotting is produced on the under surface, as there is in the case of the rhododendron bug. Mealy winged insects will be found on the highest leaves from mid June to mid July. Sooty fungi will appear on the upper surfaces of the lower leaves because of the honeydew that these insects exude. *Control Measures* Spray in September and April with a nicotine and white oil emulsion.

Formula: 1 oz nicotine, 1 pt white oil petroleum emulsion, to 10 gal. water.

Dust with either derris dust or nicotine dust in the summer when any flies are seen.

RHODODENDRON BUG (*Stephanitis rhododendri*)
The signs of the above pest are similar to those made by whitefly on the rhododendron with the addition of chocolate spots on the under sides of the leaves. *Control Measures* Spray in June and July with derris emulsion. The shrubs can be sponged with a Pysect Aerosol if preferred.

12   Soil sterilisation, and warm-water treatment of plants

One of the most successful ways in which pests and diseases which live in the soil can be controlled is by what is called soil sterilisation, though actually the term refers to the partial sterilisation of soil. The author has had considerable experience in this subject.

Partial soil sterilisation ensures that all insects, their eggs or pupa are killed; all fungi are destroyed; all weeds destroyed also, and all non-spore producing bacteria killed. The surviving ammonia-producing organisms are able to multiply in consequence, in an unrestricted manner and carry out their activities on a much larger scale immediately. Naturally, such soil is ideal for it gives almost perfect germination and much labour is saved on weeding. Further, the increased fertility of the soil, and the destruction of insect pests and diseases recompenses amply for any costs involved in the operation.

Some like to sterilise soil by means of boiling water. It takes, however, about forty gallons of boiling water to the square yard in order to reach the right temperature to a depth of ten inches. It is, therefore, a costly method and, because of the excess water used, is apt to ruin the texture of the soil.

WARM WATER TREATMENT

The warm or hot water treatment of plants however, was originally designed to destroy the grubs of the narcissus fly found in bulbs. Since that time warm water has been used to treat strawberry in order to control eelworm, tarsonemid mites, etc., and may be used for treating violets, phlox, chrysanthemum and other plants that are attacked by eelworms.

The general scheme is as follows.

The plants concerned should be immersed in water at a temperature of exactly 110°F. for twenty minutes, three degrees on either side being the safest margin. Bulbs should be treated when they are in a dormant conditions, say six weeks after lifting in the autumn and should be in the hot-water bath

for four hours. Chrysanthemum stools may be treated in the
autumn after the plants have been cut down, or the cuttings
themselves may be treated before planting. Young violet and
strawberry plants are usually treated before they are planted,
and warm-water treatment usually gives them a check for
about a fortnight; the wise gardener, therefore, tries to be done
with his planting as early as possible.

It is important to see that the whole of the water in the bath
is at the right temperature so some arrangement must be made
for seeing that the water is stirred. The thermometer must
read correctly, and it is advisable to have a false bottom to the
tank, so that the water can circulate under the bulbs or plants
that are being treated as well as over them.

Bulbs do not need to be cooled down quickly after being
taken out of the bath, but other plants do. They should be put
under a tap of cold water or plunged in a bath.

Having sterilised plants in this way it is, of course, foolish to
replant them in infected soil.

There are various baths on the market which are made especially for sterilising purposes, but the ingenious gardener
will be able to rig up his own apparatus quite cheaply.

13 Formulae of insecticides and fungicides, and details of fumigants and dusts

Throughout the book, instructions have been given as to the best insecticides or fungicides to use for the particular purpose on hand. In this chapter, definite formulae will be found with regard to the various washes and dusts to be used, together with other information that will prove useful to the gardener.

CONTACT SPRAYS
Sucking insects can only be controlled by contact sprays, for they do not eat the leaves and stems.

NICOTINE AND SOFT SOAP
Formula: 1 oz nicotine (95–98 per cent), $\frac{1}{4}$ lb. soft soap (or a spreader e.g. Shellestol), 10 gal. water. Alternative formula: $\frac{1}{2}$ oz nicotine, $\frac{3}{4}$ lb. soft soap, 10 gal. water.

The soft soap should be dissolved in a little warm water first of all and be allowed to cool. The nicotine should then be added and the solution made up to 10 gal.

PYRETHRUM EXTRACT
Can be bought as Pyrethrex or as Pysect Aerosol.

Formula: $1\frac{1}{2}$ pts concentrated extract, 100 gal. water.

PARAFFIN EMULSION
Formula: $\frac{1}{4}$ gal. paraffin, $1\frac{1}{2}$ lb. soft soap, 10 gal. water.

Boil the soap and water. Pour in the paraffin slowly while boiling, stirring all the time. Allow to cool before using.

WHITE OIL EMULSION
Highly refined petroleum oils of high boiling point may be used for controlling scale insects and red spiders.

Formula: according to instructions on container.

QUASSIA
A very safe insecticide – never kills ladybirds or bees. Quassia consists of chips of the wood of the tree *Pircrasma quassioides*

164

which will keep dry for years and can be bought from a good chemist. Boil 4 oz Quassia chips in 1 gal. water for two hours. The yellow liquid produced should be poured off when cool. Then dilute this liquid with five parts of water. Use it as an all-round garden spray for aphides and caterpillars. Excellent for controlling the gooseberry sawfly caterpillars.

RHUBARB SPRAY

For aphids on roses and other flowers. Chop up 3 lb. rhubarb leaves. Boil for $\frac{1}{2}$ hr in 6 pts water. When cool strain and dissolve 1 oz soapflakes in 2 pts water. Mix the rhubarb liquid with the soapy water and then use as a spray for any greenflies. It can also be made with 3 lb. elder leaves, and this mixture was used in the past as a spray for mildew on roses.

Dusts

NICOTINE DUST

Usually three grades, 2 per cent, 3 per cent and 4 per cent. Use 2 per cent for greenfly, use 3 per cent for capsids, greenfly and caterpillars, use 4 per cent when combined with arsenate or derris for controlling both biting and sucking insects.

Use on calm days when warm.

DERRIS DUST

Similar to derris sprays but never so effective. It is non-poisonous. Apply with dusting machine. Use liberally.

SULPHUR DUST

For controlling fungus diseases as recommended in the book. Be sure not to buy just flowers of sulphur, but buy the specially manufactured dust for this purpose.

COPPER-LIME DUST

To be used instead of Bordeaux mixture. Useful for controlling potato blight, celery blight, tulip fire, etc.

Fungicides

LIME-SULPHUR

A brownish-red liquid; purchase with a polysulphide content of 25 per cent and a specific gravity of 1.3. Use according to instructions given throughout the book.

Must not be mixed with soap. Works more effectively when used with a soapless spreader.

BORDEAUX MIXTURE

Can be bought mixed in paste form but is cheaper to make at home.

Formula: 4 lb. quicklime, 6 lb. copper sulphate, 100 gal. water, or 6 lb. quicklime, 4 lb. copper sulphate, 100 gal. water.

This latter is known as excess lime Bordeaux and is better for celery or any plants where there is a danger of damage being done by the copper.

Don't place the copper sulphate or the final mixture in a metal bucket. Slake the quicklime gradually with a little water and then add the rest of the water. Dissolve the copper sulphate overnight. Pour this into the lime gradually, stirring all the time. It is possible to buy Bordeaux Paste ready for diluting with water. (Other formulas used with fruit trees are found in the text dealing with diseases.)

LIVER OF SULPHUR

Formula: 5 oz liver of sulphate, $\frac{1}{2}$ lb. soft soap, 10 gal. water.

COLLOIDAL SULPHUR

Liquid sulphur in a very finely divided state. Usually sold as Sulsol.

COLLOIDAL BORDEAUX

Liquid Bordeaux in a finely divided state. N.B. Use proprietary forms according to instructions on container.

BURGUNDY MIXTURE

Formula: 8 oz copper sulphate, 10 oz washing soda, 5 gal. water.

Dissolve copper sulphate in 4 gal. water and washing soda in 1 gal. Pour washing soda solution slowly into copper sulphate solution, and stir all the time. Use at once and keep agitated. It is safer to use wooden or enamel vessels.

ELDERBERRY LEAVES

Boil 3 lb. Elderberry leaves in 6 pts water and 1 oz. soap flakes and use to control mildew on roses and Michaelmas daisies.

Cleansing Trees in Winter

CAUSTIC SODA

Old-fashioned wash for trees. Still used sometimes late in winter against brown rot.

Formula: 1 lb. caustic soda, 10 gal. water.

DINITRO-ORTHO-CRESOL EMULSION

Popularly called DNC this is a combined wash of dinitro-ortho-cresol and petroleum oil. By means of this spray the complete winter wash programme can be carried out in one operation. It is particularly effective against fruit tree red spider, apple capsid bug and the common green capsid, used at a strength of 4–7 per cent. DNC gives only partial control of the eggs of the winter moth group, and so in this case it must be followed by a lead arsenate spray at the green 'cluster' stage of bud development.

OVARMORT SPECIAL 'A'

A combined DNC *petroleum* winter wash having insecticidal, ovicidal and certain fungicidal properties on fruit crops.

Top bush and cane fruits for the control of over-wintering stages of aphids, suckers, red spider mites, winter moths, capsids and raspberry moth. In addition reduction of scab and primary mildew infections. The reduction of mildewed leaf-trusses and shoots is highest when the application is made in December.

Use 4 per cent HV on all crops. Apples may be treated at 9 per cent.

Soil Sterilent

CHESHUNT COMPOUND

Formula: 2 parts by weight copper sulphate, 11 parts by weight ammonium carbonate.

Crush the ammonium carbonate to a powder. Mix with the powdered copper sulphate and store in tightly corked jar for 24 hours before using. Prepare the solution by dissolving 1 oz of the dry mixture in a little hot water and then adding 2 gal. of water. Use iron or tin containers and only prepare just as much as is needed for immediate use.

FORMALIN

A 2 per cent solution is used for disinfecting the wood of empty glasshouses and frames and for washing pots and boxes. It is also used for sterilising soil.

Spreaders

It is usual when mixing sprays to add a spreader to increase the efficiency of the spray and make it easier to apply.

Various spreaders are:

1. *Soap* Useless as a spreader with such washes as Bordeaux, lead arsenate and lime-sulphur, but commonly used with nicotine. Normally 10 lb. soft soap per 100 gal. water.

2. *Calcium caseinate* Used chiefly with lime-sulphur at the rate of $2\frac{1}{2}$ lb. to 100 gal. water.

3. *Saponin* Use at the rate of 2 oz per 100 gal. water.

4. *Estol H.* A proprietary spreader. Use in accordance with instructions on the bottle. Has given excellent results. Now called Shellestol.

Fumigants

NAPHTHALENE

Use either in the crude form as whizzed naphthalene or in the white crystalline form as flaked naphthalene.

Formula: Light soils: 3 oz per sq. yd. Heavy soils: 6 oz per sq. yd.

Spread evenly, fork in thoroughly. Water copiously.

Will drive away wireworms, millipedes, root maggots, woodlice, root-feeding aphides and other larvae.

NAPHTHALENE, Grade 16

Used under glass to control red spiders and thrips.

Vaporise over special lamps.

Formula: 4–6 oz grade 16 naphthalene to 1,000 cu. ft.

Fumigate after house has been damped down in the evening. Continue for 12 hours. Keep temperature at 70°F.

In bad cases of thrip on carnations, cyclamen and arums, this grade naphthalene should be broadcast at the rate of 10 oz per 1,000 cu. ft.

CARBON BI-SULPHIDE

Highly inflammable. Don't smoke when using.

Formula: Make holes with crowbar or stake 2 ft deep, pour in chemical at rate of 2 oz per cu. ft. Cover each hole immediately to conserve fumes.

Useful for heaps of soil. Will control wireworms, chafer larvae, root aphides, ants.

NICOTINE

Fumigant for glass houses. May be used as 'shreds' or liquid. It is poisonous.

Formula: $\frac{1}{8}$ fl. oz methylated spirit to 1,000 cu. ft of space.

Vaporise in small pan placed over spirit lamp.

PARADICHLORBENZENE

This is effective against wireworms. Break it up into portions about the size of a French bean and bury these in holes 6 ins. deep and 2 ft apart, closing the holes when the chemical is in position with the heel of your boot.

DAZOMET

A soil fumigant and sterilant.

Applied 2 oz to the sq. yd and forked into the soil when it is 50°F or above. This will do its work in one month to six weeks. Should be watered or rolled after forking well. When the time is up, fork the ground over to release fumes and the soil will be ready to plant. Very thorough sterilising takes place, and it is advisable to test with radish seed to ensure that all fumes have gone. As its name implies, it is built up round an organic nitrogen molecule, and therefore leaves the ground more enriched.

14   Harmless and beneficial insects

It will be quite a relief to readers of this book to know that there are a very large number of harmless and even beneficial insects. It would be a pity not to end a book of this kind on a bright note and it is hoped, therefore, that chapter 14 will help to cheer gardeners up who may be depressed as the result of wading through the many injurious pests and diseases there are.

There are a number of insects, for instance, that are called predaceous. That is to say, they live by feeding on insect pests. Ladybirds are perhaps the best known of these. The two common species being the 7-spot and the 2-spot ladybird beetles. They feed on greenfly, red spiders and on the scale insects.

Now most people recognise ladybirds but unfortunately they fail to recognise the young which are commonly called niggers. These niggers are, as their name suggests, black, and may have little round spots on their backs. They are a little bit longer than a ladybird, a little bit less wide and not so 'high'. They look like tiny little alligators.

Do not destroy ladybirds or the niggers and, in fact, encourage them all you can.

Another predaceous insect is the hover-fly . Perhaps you have often seen, as you go down a path, a little fly smaller than a wasp, of a similar colour, hovering in the air and remaining stationary. As you approach, it may dart to one side, and continue to hover, its little wings seeming to beat thousands of times per minute. These are particularly abundant on warm days. They lay their eggs on leaves and shoots where aphides (greenflies) are feeding. Tiny little reddish-green or green slug-like maggots emerge which feed on the aphides.

Sow a row of Buckwheat in April in between the Brussels sprouts in your vegetable garden. The hover or chalcid wasps love the tiny white flowers and feed on the pollen and nectar. Each larva of the wasps consumes 600 aphides before it becomes an adult.

Another plant the Hover Fly loves is the *Royal Ensign* variety of the Convolvulus tricolor. Sow the seeds in April also.

Lace-wing flies, sometimes called fly-goldings, are lovely

Ladybird larva on rosebud. The larva preys on aphids
(George E. Hyde)

little fragile insects which have light-green bodies and four lace-patterned wings. They are very fond of greenfly and they feed voraciously on woolly aphides. Their eggs are very noticeable for they are attached to long, thread-like stalks and may be found anywhere where greenflies congregate.

They sway readily in the wind. The grubs that hatch out suck the body juices of the insects.

There are capsid bugs which are destructive to pests. They will feed on tortrix caterpillars, and other caterpillars too; on red spiders and on aphides, and when other food is scarce, they will eat one another.

There are small, flattish red bugs which look something like tiny capsid bugs and are often erroneously called red spiders. These large red bugs feed on the red spiders and suck their eggs dry. Its proper name is the anthocorid bug.

There are numbers of ground beetles and rove beetles which are most useful to the gardener. The devil's coach-horse beetle, for instance, devours hundreds of harmful insects in a year. It is recognised by its habit of cocking its tail up into the air.

Sometimes I am asked how to tell a 'good' insect from a harmful insect, and the only rule of thumb method I can suggest is that the good insects at their grub or caterpillar stages are very active, while the harmful insects, on the whole, are more sluggish.

Another mite is known as the red velvet mite. It is a bright velvety red and is usually found walking about the branches of fruit trees in a rather 'stately' manner. It is not a red spider and is a useful insect in that it feeds on woolly aphids. Its Latin name is *Allothrombium fuliginosum*.

Gardeners will be delighted to know that there is at least one slug which is a friend. Its Latin name is *Pestacella*. It is pale yellow in colour. Its length when moving is about 3 in., closing to about 1 in. It can be distinguished from the harmful species by the small flat shell on its tail end. It feeds on slugs and other ground creatures.

Centipedes are definitely beneficial and are distinguishable from millipedes because they have only one pair of legs to each body segment, compared with two pairs on millipedes. They are more rapid moving than millipedes, and have longer legs too.

Earthworms are, of course, beneficial and are useful aerators of the soil. They help to reduce organic matter into such a condition that it is available for plant food.

Bees are particularly useful for pollinating the blossom of fruit and during the spring and early summer, wasps are useful, too, for they feed on aphids and other small insects, taking them to their nests. Later, however, they feed on the fruit, and their nests should then be destroyed.

The greenhouse whitefly parasite is *Encarsia formosa*, or chalcid wasp. It lays eggs in the young of the whitefly, the larvae that hatch out feeding on the whitefly scales and causing them to turn black. It is fairly easy to set up a colony of these predaceous insects in a greenhouse.

One of the most interesting parasites is that of the cabbage caterpillar (*Apanteles glomeratus*). This Icheumen fly lays its eggs in the young caterpillars, the larvae of which feed inside, thus killing them. The larvae then emerge as yellow cocoons; the gardener, therefore, should never destroy caterpillars surrounded by such cocoons.

NOTES ON BEES
Insecticides can harm bees by killing them when (1) the spray

falls on the bees at work in a crop; (2) by the bees coming into contact with surfaces that have been sprayed with a poison and (3) if the bees drink poisoned water or nectar or eat poisoned pollen they die.

Other beneficial pollinating and predatory insects may also be poisoned by direct contact or by residual action as well as, of course, by ingestion of the poison.

BHC dieldrin and demeton-methyl are highly toxic to bees, but others can be toxic also. Lime sulphur, copper and mercury fungicides are comparatively harmless to bees, however.

Bees and other pollinating insects are likely to be abundant where and when there is open blossom; dusts and sprays should not be applied at that time. This applies not only to the particular crop sprayed, but to other flowers in the vicinity, including weed and hedgerow blossoms, on which the spray or dust may settle. Sprays are preferable to dusts because some of the 'fillers' used in dust formulations are toxic.

In some areas there is a voluntary bee warning scheme in May and June.

Biological control

Various methods of using a whitefly parasite *Encarsia formosa* and the red spider mite *Phytoseiulus persimilis*.

CUCUMBERS

Introduce the whitefly scales at 10 to every fifth plant. Fourteen days later introduce parasitised scales at the rate of 20 per plant. If whitefly is present already it is not necessary to introduce it. In the case of the red spider mite introduce the red spider mites on bean leaves at 10 to every plant. Introduce two predators to each alternate plant about ten days later.

TOMATOES

Introduce the whiteflies at 10 per plant in the propagating house. Introduce the parasite at 38–50 per plant to one plant in 100 in the propagating house about fourteen days before planting in the greenhouse. Then introduce the parasite as follows – three weeks after planting 150 per plant; 5 weeks after planting 150 per plant; 9 weeks after planting 75 per plant. This gives a total of 413 per plant to 1 plant in 100.

WHITEFLY PRESENT IN THE GREENHOUSE
IN SMALL NUMBERS

Introduce the parasite at 1 per plant on about five occasions at 2 week intervals until black parasitised scales appear in crop.

15 Recognition

Recognition of the whitefly and of the parasite

THE WHITEFLY (*Trialeurodes vaporariorum*)
Adults are gregarious and collect in vast numbers on the young leaves and at the tops of the plants. The wax on the wings gives them a pure white coloration.

The eggs are very small and elongated. They are attached to leaf by a short stalk. They start by being yellowish and become black after two days.

The female lives about 21 days and lays some 200 eggs at the rate of 5–8 a day. These hatch in 12 days at 64°F or in 8 days at 70°F. The complete life cycle takes 3 weeks at 70°F or 7 weeks at 64°F.

The adults and scales suck and remove liquid from leaves. They excrete honeydew on which a black sooty mould grows. They attack a very wide range of plants under glass. The adults will fly actively if disturbed. Immature stages do not move.

THE PARASITE
The adults have dark-brown heads, black thoraxes and yellow abdomens. The Ovipositor extends conspicuously beyond tip of abdomen.

The eggs are laid within whitefly scale. Usually a fairly mature scale is selected and one egg laid within. If the parasites are very numerous the scales will be punctured many times and will not develop further.

The female lives 14–21 days or only 4–5 days if no honeydew is available as food. She lays about 60–100 eggs usually one egg per whitefly scale. These hatch out in four days. The larvae feeds eight days and then pupates within scale which becomes black. The adult emerges ten days later. The life cycle is 30 days at 70°F and 6 weeks at 64°F.

The adult feeds on honeydew excreted by adult and in the immature stages of whitefly.

The adults are very active on the leaves, seeking out the

Caterpillar killed by parasitical larvae (George E. Hyde)

whitefly scales in which the eggs are laid. The adults can fly quite actively.

Recognition of the red spiders and of the predators

RED SPIDER (*Tetranychus telarius*)
The adult female red spider mite is greenish in colour with dark markings on the body. The legs dark and not obvious – summer form. The over-wintering female is deep red in colour.

The eggs are very small and completely circular white or pinkish in colour.

The female lives three weeks and lays about 120 eggs at the rate of 7–10 per day. These hatch out in five days and the complete life cycle (egg to adult) takes about fourteen days. The mites feed on a wide range of plants.

The red spiders are rather slow moving, except when temperatures exceed 75°F. When they are present in very large numbers, dense webs are formed.

THE PREDATORS

The adult female is shiny orange-brown in colour. The legs long and rather pale. It does not hibernate. In the absence of red spider mites it will starve to death.

The eggs are large and oval, usually pale brown in colour.

The female lives three weeks and lays 50–60 eggs at the rate of 3–4 per day. They hatch in 2–3 days and the complete life cycle (egg to adult) takes about seven days.

The predator feeds on red spider mite only and at the rate of 5 adult or 20 young mites or up to 30 eggs per day.

The predators are very active when searching for the red spider mite. Front pair of legs move very quickly – in fact, they may be likened to the antennae-feelers of insects.

Suppliers of biological control agents for greenhouse pests

Lesley C. Scopes,
3 South Road,
Felpham,
Sussex PO22 8EF.

Predators on plant material. *Encarsia formosa* – the whitefly parasite, on leaves.

Biological Control Unit,
University of Exeter,
Hatherly Laboratories,
Prince of Wales Road,
Exeter EX4 4PS.

Predators on plant material. *Encarsia formosa* – the whitefly parasite on plant leaves.

Organic Farmers and
Growers Ltd,
Longridge,
Creeting Road,
Stowmarket,
Suffolk IP14 5BT.

Predators on plant material. *Encarsia formosa* – the whitefly parasite supplied on plant material.